02. 04. 2006

Neal,

Since you wash some of the buildings that I have learned about in architecture school, inspire me to design, and even the one that I live in – I had to get you a copy of my new favorite book! If you want a "window" to my style as a designer – this book is it! Chicago, the place where the skyscraper was born, their legacy, in part, is left to you. You should think of yourself as an architectural preservationist!

Thank you so much for everything.

It is such a pleasure to be your friend.

Happy 40th Birthday!

[illegible]

HIGH-RISE LIVING

HIGH-RISE LIVING

ANDREW WEAVING

Gibbs Smith, Publisher
Salt Lake City

DEDICATION

For Christian Browne, risen high, watching over us.

ACKNOWLEDGEMENTS

I'd like to thank everyone who helped make this book happen, beginning with Christopher Robbins at Gibbs Smith, Publisher, who gave me the chance to complete this project, and everyone else there who has been so enthusiastic and encouraging from the start.

There are many others who have helped in the process, though, too many to mention all. Special thanks go to Debra Colman in Chicago for her help in scouting great locations there; Don Powell, Johnny Navin, Leslie Bodenstein and Mario Aranda, also in Chicago, for their time and enthusiasm. For allowing us into their homes: Michael Pado and Alice Adams at Lake Shore Drive; Larry Converso at Marina City; Judy Ross, The Moderns, Kathleen DeFouw, Kim Hastreiter, and John Mulling in New York; and in London, thanks especially to Simon Andrews for the tour of his home and its surroundings.

Thanks to everyone at various architectural offices throughout the world that have supplied information and images for use in this book and helped to make this an interesting and informative publication to both the architecture addict and the high-rise dweller.

And at home, always good to get back to, many thanks to Ian and Gretel, who have put up with my piles of papers and photos throughout the working time of this book and hopefully are now looking forward to my next project.

First Edition

08 07 06 05 04 5 4 3 2 1

Photograph credits on page 176

Published by
Gibbs Smith, Publisher
P.O. Box 667
Layton, Utah 84041

1.800.748.5439 orders
www.gibbs-smith.com

Designed by Tom Sieu and John Barretto
Printed and bound in Hong Kong

Library of Congress Cataloging-in-Publication Data

Weaving, Andrew.
High-rise living / Andrew Weaving.—1st ed.

p. cm.

Includes bibliographical references.

ISBN 1-58685-410-0

1. High-rise apartment buildings. 2. Apartments-Remodeling.
3. Interior decoration. I. Title.

NA7860.W33 2004

728'.314—dc22

2004004834

ISBN 1-58685-410-0

CONTENTS

PREFACE

Whenever I think about where I'd like to move to, living high-rise is always near the top of the list. The selection of buildings and locations to choose from is vast. Many high-rise residential buildings are being built in the Canary Wharf area of London, where I live in a vintage loft space. My view is an urban landscape of old and new buildings. From my windows I look at Goldfinger's Balfron Tower and the Millennium Dome. I can also see the new high-rise complex by Skidmore, Owings and Merrill, where at least three new office towers are going up. There is a vast array of large new complexes of urban living in various other parts of the world as well, from Vancouver to Tokyo, New York to London. For most people, these buildings are ideal. The apartments are complete, the facilities are easily available, the utilities work, and the locations are usually prime.

But if I were to move into a high-rise, it would have to be a vintage building. The Barbican in London would be my first choice, although, as I have many clients and customers who live there, I know that the service charges—which cover everything from the concierge to the heat and air, from the window cleaning to the car parking—are quite high. But it is great to be able to visit these apartments to see how people reinterpret them, from the purist who wants to restore every detail, to the contemporary dweller who wants to bring the whole thing up to date. I do find very frustrating, though, the cases where new owners, who have bought a completely original space, tear out all the fittings, kitchens, and bathrooms and install anonymous "updated" versions that are completely dated as soon as they are fitted. Some designs are timeless. It is a visionary and high-minded home-dweller who will keep the original classical elements and only add new accessories with judgment to bring it up to date.

The main problem in the U.K. is that most of the great high-rise buildings were built by local authorities as a low-cost-rent alternative for local people. Many high-rises are now privately owned, which results in only a small percentage of the apartments being owned rather than rented. One other problem here is that it is sometimes difficult to raise a mortgage on these older buildings due to their construction method and also the percentage of rental units; mortgage lenders in the U.K. will not lend money on buildings over five stories tall if they were local-authority owned or built. I have spoken to many of these authorities and they will not or cannot explain. However, these policies are slowly changing due to popular demand and the fact that more and more high-rise residential buildings are being built.

While in Chicago shooting the stories for this book, I met some great residents of the Mies van der Rohe high-rise blocks. In 910 Diversey, I met two sisters who have lived in the Commonwealth Promenade Apartments since the '50s, when it was built. Their apartment, a slight step back in time, is immaculate, and they love their great views of Lincoln Park and the city beyond. Where else would be better to live? In 860 Lake Shore Drive, I met the gent who had dressed the Rat Pack. It is encouraging for younger generations that there is still such support and enthusiasm for these places, and that they still exist. In the updated versions of 910 Diversey that I have included in this book, the apartments have been well reinterpreted—in the words of Chicago-based architect Mario Aranda, "reclassicized." Although the Mies buildings do appeal to a select group (the bathrooms are small, the windows are not double-glazed, the service charges can be high, and in some cases the ceilings quite low), how else can you afford a piece of classic architecture by a master of design, a limited-edition unit that you can add your mark to?

High-rise dwellers throughout the world are much the same: they want to live in something great, to be part of the community—their neighborhood in the sky—and live comfortably in a unit well designed for twenty-first-century living.

RIGHT PAGE / THE EVER-GROWING NEW LONDON DOCKLANDS SKYLINE.

HSBC

INTRODUCTION

High-rise architecture has provided some of the **most technically innovative** and **aesthetically interesting** buildings of recent years, though its history is checkered and often controversial. Since its beginnings within the modernist movement in the 1920s as a **utopian ideal** based on socialist principles, through the realization of many schemes from the 1950s onward, when developers and local authorities embraced many of its architectural principles, to its current re-evaluation and **resurgence in popularity**—at no time more than now has the high-rise enjoyed such an appreciative audience. The choice of high-rise living space available to the newest generation of city dwellers—from renovated and transformed classic public housing to the growing spread of light, airy new apartments—is considered some of the **most desirable property available in cities** throughout the world.

LEFT PAGE / THESE LATE-'50s TWELVE-STORY BLOCKS, AS SEEN FROM MY OFFICE DESK, ARE ABOUT TO BE DEMOLISHED TO MAKE WAY FOR LOCAL REDEVELOPMENT. BUILT QUICKLY TO REHOUSE THOSE EVACUATED DURING WWII, THIS TYPE OF BUILDING IS TYPICAL OF INNER-CITY PUBLIC HOUSING.

This sea of change in attitudes toward high-rise living was perhaps inevitable. Modernism in its many forms has been rediscovered by a new generation that has come to appreciate a design aesthetic that, some ten to fifteen years ago, had only a limited audience. At the same time there is a huge resurgence of desire to live centrally in the city. As urban populations continue to expand and necessary environmental restrictions on building sites persist, the current impulse—and only real solution to the increasing demand for city housing—is to build higher. The urban high-rise apartment provides the perfect solution: a modern, architecturally designed space in which to live, right in the heart of the city.

The high-rise has not always been held in such high esteem. It has, however, always been a way of providing multiunit housing in increasingly congested urban environments. It has also offered architects huge scope and the opportunity to design unified, large-scale structures flexible enough for a wide range of specific use. Although the results in many, often well-documented, cases have been disappointing and inadequate, when the design and purpose have worked, the effects have been profound: **their influence on the way we will be living in the future is incalculable.**

It all really started with the work of Boston-born architect **Louis Sullivan** in the **1890s.** Previous to this date, Sullivan, with German engineer Dankmar Adler, was building in masonry. This meant that buildings could only be a certain height due to the weight of the materials. Although in 1881, Burnham and Root, an American duo, built the Monadnock building in Chicago that managed to get to seventeen stories tall, its walls at ground level were at least twelve feet thick. In 1890, Sullivan and Adler built their first building using "skyscraper construction"—the Wainwright Building in St. Louis, Missouri—by applying an external material, such as masonry, to an internal steel skeleton, with bolts. Soon after, the use of steel frame with external sheathing became commonplace. But it was Louis Sullivan who said that buildings must be tall, soaring things, rising in sheer exultation. At this time his main draftsman was none other than a young Frank Lloyd Wright. Of course, Wright went on to build his low-level suburban dwellings, but with his later ideas for the Price Tower and the mile-high Illinois Tower, working in this urban environment must have made an impression on his work.

ABOVE / CARSON PIRIE & SCOTT DEPARTMENT STORE, CHICAGO: THE FORERUNNER OF MANY MODERN HIGH-RISE BLOCKS OF THE TWENTIETH CENTURY.

The draw to taller buildings had hit Europe, too. In France, **Auguste Perret** and Tony Garnier were coming up with buildings using reinforced concrete to create great expanses of what looked like unsupported floors and ceilings. As early as 1899 Perret and his brother Gustav were using reinforced concrete (concrete reinforced with steel rods) for buildings with spans of fifty feet or so. It allowed for simpler and undecorated structures. As with other art nouveau buildings of similar times, the concrete and stone were carved and molded like clay to give the impression of natural organic forms. However, the appearance of their later buildings is as drastically different in appearance from their early buildings as the difference between Beaux-Arts and art nouveau.

In 1902 Perret built a block of flats in Paris. At 25 bis, rue Franklin he built a tall building with a concrete skeletal frame that allowed for great flexibility in its planning. The internal layout was free-flowing, like those of Le Corbusier's later work. All the main living rooms opened onto each other. Because of the location of this building, one would expect it to be adorned with art nouveau, but no. This building, with its very exposed structure, is uninfluenced by anything around it. It is decorated with ceramic tiles and some floral stonework but on first impression it is a very simple, basic form.

Tony Garnier had plans. His Cité Industrielle, a plan for the perfect socialist city without private property, churches, courts of law, etc., and whose

foundation would be industry, was initially put together as early as 1901, and continued to be developed over the next decade. Though unpublished until 1918, his Cité Industrielle was known to other architects, and influenced further city planning. The ideas formed here became the basis of the slightly later ideal-city plans by others, such as **Le Corbusier** and **Yorke and Breuer.** Yorke and Breuer's scheme of **1936** was a model commissioned by the British Cement and Concrete Association. This project for a new city's ideals were "to free the town from congestion, to let sunlight and clean air penetrate freely between buildings, so that the town is a pleasant and healthy place to live and work." The twelve-story residential towers were placed far enough apart to allow sunlight to penetrate the buildings. Le Corbusier's ideas for La Ville Radieuse, another ideal-city plan produced slightly earlier than Yorke and Breuer's, included a plan to have the entire ground level of the new city for the use of the pedestrian. All traffic was to be raised above the ground and all the buildings were to be built on *pilotis,* or columns, with great distances between them so there would be unrestricted views for all. This plan would house 400 people per acre. The Unité d'Habitation saw this plan fulfilled to some extent, but instead of building groups of blocks placed together, the Unité d'Habitation was a block built singly and reproduced in various locations throughout Europe.

ABOVE / THIS APARTMENT BLOCK IN PARIS WAS BUILT WITH A SIMPLE CONCRETE FRAME, ENABLING LARGE WINDOWS AND SPACIOUS INTERIORS.

In the U.S.A., **Frank Lloyd Wright** was on his own, building more and more individual houses for the ever-increasing number of admirers of his style. But while it was all happening, in the middle of a building boom in the United States, Wright's work slowed down. Some believed this would be the end of his career.

Though he had designed and planned many high-rise projects, few were ever built. His **Price Tower** in Bartlesville, Oklahoma, was one of the few and it took twenty-five years to come to fruition, having been designed in 1928 but not built until **1953.**

Also in the U.S.A., **Richard Neutra** came up with a scheme for a utopian city named **Rush City Reformed**, a complete city with skyscrapers, low-rise schools, etc. Can you imagine a Neutra house twelve or so stories high? This was used to illustrate a book by Neutra titled *Wie Baut Amerika? (How America Builds.)* Published in Germany in **1927**, the book sold well throughout the world, and included ideas on problems relating to North American architecture and urban design. It included many illustrations and photographs of works in progress and new building methods and materials. Rush City Reformed was the name given to a series of urban designs Neutra came up with for Berlin, New York, Chicago, and Wisconsin. With the label "Rush City" you get the image of living in the fast lane during the boom time coming to these cities. In his drawings, Neutra highlighted the importance of transport, by rail and car. There were high-level bridges and roads amongst low-rise housing for families with children and high-rise towers for workers. This scheme included schools, community centers, drive-in markets, and train terminals. The overall appearance of Rush City Reformed reflected the high-rises of Chicago and the low urban sprawl of Los Angeles. For Neutra, who built many

ABOVE / INITIALLY DESIGNED FOR A MANHATTAN LOCATION IN THE 1920s, PRICE TOWER WAS NOT ACTUALLY BUILT UNTIL THE MID-'50s, AND THEN, IN BARTLESVILLE, OKLAHOMA.

low-rise apartment blocks in the U.S., especially Los Angeles, this scheme for a whole city would never be realized, but it did give him a lifetime of ideas and possible solutions for problems arising from architecture and urban design.

The **Bauhaus** brought about a radical change in the way we looked at things: a building is to live in as a chair is to sit on. While at the Bauhaus, Berlin-born **Walter Gropius** worked on the school's buildings—the student and teacher housing, the educational buildings, the workshops, etc.—including the principal's house. As principal of the Bauhaus, this house was for Gropius himself. The building's design foreshadowed the way his urban-planning ideas would develop. It wasn't until he left the Bauhaus, in **1928,** that he was able to get back into his architectural practice full-time and develop his ideas for bigger schemes and town planning. Later, the buildings by Gropius included plans and models for slab-built apartment blocks. There was a scheme for fifteen blocks, housing more than 600 families, to be built in Berlin. The plans included a restaurant, rooftop solarium, and parking areas. Although many of these plans were developed, unfortunately none were built. Gropius built many low-rise developments and also worked on changing the structure of cities.

Stuttgart's **Weissenhof Seidlung exhibition of 1927,** exhibited a modern housing unit built to showcase the latest work from the biggest names in architecture. While there were no tall apartment blocks, the ideas of group housing, unit housing, and identical housing came about. Under the directorship of **Ludvig Mies van der Rohe,** the list of architects included J. J. P. Oud, Mart Stam, Hans Scharoun, Peter Behrens, Le Corbusier, Walter Gropius, and Hans Poelzig, all of whom had made their mark on the international architectural scene. The Weissenhof estate was to include a selection of housing groups and apartments for a middle-class generation. Because the architect group was so well selected, the overall appearance—thirty-three houses and apartments unified by their white, cubic forms—was one of stylistic harmony. Many of the Weissenhof Seidlung exhibition housing projects were to be the forerunners of various estates all over Europe. The Mies apartment block, for instance, four units wide by four units high, could easily be built into a sixteen-story building later on.

Another group of architects, put together this time by Gropius, created the ideal apartment: the **Siemenstadt** apartment complex of **1929–30,** near Berlin. Siemens, an electrical-appliance manufacturing company, took great responsibility for their workers and had this scheme put together for them, including many recreational facilities. The blocks designed by Gropius consisted of four stories on a north/south aspect, capturing the best of the daylight. With this scheme, at last Gropius could bring his urban-development ideas to fruition.

In England in the '30s, émigré architects such as Serge Chermayeff, Erich Mendelson, **Berthold Lubetkin,** and Marcel Breuer were building individual houses as well as apartment blocks. Breuer went on to the United States along with Chermayeff. Lubetkin, on the other hand, carried on working in the U.K. He built high-rise apartments for the private sector and the local authority. **Highpoint I and II, 1933–38,** where he lived, are desirable places to live even now. Though only eight stories high, they were one of the highest places to live at that time. Le Corbusier wrote a piece praising Highpoint I and called it the "world's first vertical garden city." This building incorporated Corb's five points of modern architecture, namely, a free facade, a free-flowing plan, strip windows, *pilotis,* and, of course, a roof garden. For the London County Council Lubetkin built a few very well-planned housing groups, some of which were high-rise.

ABOVE / MIES VAN DER ROHE'S APARTMENT BLOCK FOR THE WEISSENHOF SEIDLUNG EXHIBITION IN STUTTGART, WITH ITS LARGE EXPANSES OF GLASS, CREATED THE IDEAL APARTMENT.

Wells Coates, a Canadian working in the U.K., built a few large modernist apartment blocks—white-painted steel windows—for the private sector, and had, at the time, a very small following. His building, **Embassy Court,** built in **1935** in Brighton, on the south coast of England, resembled in some ways the reinforced-concrete block **Lawn Road Flats (Isokon Flats)** that he had built in London previously. The Lawn Road Flats building, located in Hampstead, was a monolithic block that became a commune for many fellow architects, artists, and writers. The block epitomized the "ideal flat" with its simple, built-in furniture. Jack Pritchard, who commissioned the building, lived in the penthouse of this block for many years.

Although the Second World War put a stop to architectural development in Europe, after the war, the rebuilding carried on the modern style. Schemes and plans put together by Gropius and his contemporaries became the basis for many developments being constructed at this time in Europe, where the rebuilding of many cities was taking place. The new housing de rigeur, however, was sprawling low-rise estates rather than high-rise towers.

In contrast, the war did not really put a stop to building in the U.S.A. In the mid-'40s Mies started to build his Promontory Apartments. These buildings of two- or three-bedroom configurations were constructed of an exposed, reinforced-concrete frame with concrete slab floors, suspended plaster ceilings, and sliding windows with aluminum sashes. The block of some twenty floors had 122 flats. Despite its innovative looks, the Promontory Apartments building appears quite traditional with its brick infills and low, wide window arrangements, in contrast to Mies van der Rohe's famous Lake Shore Drive Apartments, built later, between 1948 and 1951. These latter are very similar in form but their steel frame and glass inserts accentuate the soaring element. Their elevation gives the impression of an endless tower of Farnsworth House elements—an interior that is open and spacious, and an exterior whose flat skeleton is framed with glass panes suspended in space.

Back in France, **Le Corbusier** was building his **Unité d'Habitation** of **1946–52:** reinforced-concrete blocks of about 300 apartments raised on *pilotis.* His "ideal city" built at last, but on an individual scale, the blocks included all the Corbusian details one would expect: everything built-in, everything designed specifically for its use. There were five of these blocks built throughout Europe. With these schemes, Corbusier saw

ABOVE / LUBETKIN'S HIGHPOINT I. THE MONOLITHIC APARTMENT BLOCK, WITH HIGHPOINT II BEHIND IT, WAS THE FIRST OF ITS TYPE IN THE U.K.

ABOVE / WELLS COATES' EMBASSY COURT ON THE SOUTH COAST OF ENGLAND RESEMBLES AN OCEAN LINER AND INCLUDES SEVENTY OR SO APARTMENTS OF VARIOUS SIZES AND FORMATS.

himself as a sort of social reformer, giving the city order with great buildings, open parks, and trees. This building included a hotel, barber shops, and a whole shopping "street" halfway up the building so that you didn't have to go too far for whatever you wanted.

In the United States, more **Mies** blocks were being built. They were hip: this is where you wanted to live. **Frank Lloyd Wright** shocked America when he came up with the idea of the **mile-high Illinois Tower,** which relied on the tap-root system—a deeply embedded concrete foundation, similar to the tap-root of a tree, from which everything was cantilevered. A whole city, again in one building, it was to be over 500 stories tall—more than four times the height of the Empire State Building. It was only a concept but it certainly got architects thinking. With a taproot foundation used successfully in previous projects, such as the S.C. Johnson Research Tower, it was at this time, 1952, that the **Price Tower** was at last built.

Elsewhere in the U.S.A., other schemes of public housing were being designed and built. In 1905, at the age of four, Louis I. Kahn arrived in Philadelphia, where he would build many of his major works. Kahn had great input in solving the public housing problems with his schemes that included both high- and low-rise buildings. Two of these were Mill Creek I (1952–53) and Mill Creek II (1959–62). A group of other architects, including Carl Koch and Ralph Rapson, built a rambling twelve-story complex in Cambridge, Massachusetts. Financed by the New England Mutual Life Insurance Company, the scheme included over 250 flats, each with a large balcony overlooking the Charles River. In 1956, Skidmore, Owings and Merrill came up with a scheme to redevelop a very high-density slum area in South Chicago. Created for middle-income families, the blocks consisted of five twelve-story and four twenty-one-story buildings of reinforced-concrete, flat-slab construction. The Lake Meadows Apartments had full-width windows facing north and south and, like so many of the new schemes, included schools, churches, shopping centers, a medical center, and a park, all within close proximity to the apartment buildings.

Once Britain could start to build again, more and more high-rises went up, some good some bad—time would tell. **The London County Council** looked to Le Corbusier's vision when working on the **Roehampton** scheme, completed between **1952 and 1958.** The scheme, over 2,000 dwellings surrounded by a massive park of mature trees, was to house more than 6,500 people. Including a shopping center, schools, a library, and other amenities, this small city, with its proximity to one of Outer London's largest parks, gave the designers many worries—they were required to protect the guarded amenities of the park while creating a balance of open parkland and development. The one-hundred-foot height limit was imposed so as to give clear views to all of the park and beyond.

ABOVE / MIES VAN DER ROHE'S LAKE SHORE DRIVE APARTMENTS IS PROBABLY THE MOST WELL-KNOWN HIGH-RISE RESIDENTIAL SCHEME IN THE WORLD.

ABOVE / LE CORBUSIER'S UNITÉ D'HABITATION AT MARSEILLE. OF THE SEVERAL BUILT, THIS WAS THE MOST SUCCESSFUL. HERE THE DIVISION OF THE BUILDING WITH THE INCORPORATED "MAIN STREET" OF SHOPS AND SERVICES, IS HIGHLIGHTED BEHIND A CONCRETE SCREEN WALL.

In the mid-sixties, **Erno Goldfinger** at last had a chance to get his ideas for high-rise living developed. The Greater London Council commissioned **Balfron (1964–72)** in the east and **Trellick (1966–72)** in the west of London which were, when they were built, some of the tallest buildings in Europe. Twenty-seven and thirty-one floors high, the two towers were grouped with low-rise dwellings and community facilities. There were at least nine different unit configurations, loosely based on Le Corbusier's Unité; the units stretch from the back to the front of the building and have windows at both ends, and range from two-room low-rise flats for the elderly, to large duplex flats in the high-rises for larger families. The materials used in these buildings—beautifully finished bush-hammered concrete, marble entrance lobbies with timber brise soleils dividing the balcony areas—make it easy to understand why the blocks are still so popular with their residents.

Denys Lasdun, using different building methods, built his **"cluster blocks,"** perfected at Keeling House, in London's east end. Two towers were built, one of eight floors housing twenty-four units, and the larger, fifteen floors with sixty-four units. This larger scheme was bought by a private developer who remodeled and upgraded it so that it is now a classic piece of modern architecture summing up the whole desire to live high-rise.

In London, **Chamberlin, Powell and Bon** were planning a city-within-a-city: The Barbican development, with its four

tower blocks, groups of low-rises, houses, art and entertainment center, indoor gardens, restaurants, and gymnasium, was built under the hand of the London County Council. The Barbican had the best views of London and, as it was built for city workers who most probably went to their house in the country for the weekend, you could live here for a small weekly fee. Chamberlin, Powell and Bon had already built another development called Golden Lane in two stages on an adjacent site. This group of now-landmark buildings, including a sixteen-story apartment block of about 120 units and groups of low-rise duplex-type units, are still forward-looking in appearance.

Alvar Aalto built the first of his very few high-rise buildings, the Paimio Sanatorium, in his native Finland, in the '30s. The **Neue Vahr** building, built in Germany, where Aalto constructed much of his work, between '59 and '62, is said to be one of the best postwar housing blocks in Europe. This fan-shaped block built of prefabricated concrete blocks stands twenty-two stories high. On each floor, nine apartments, each with a different plan, have a glazed wall in the living area opening onto a private terrace. The fan-shaped plan meant that each terrace had privacy, and that the view from every apartment was different. This building for "social-collective living" housed a communal space on each floor, a roof terrace for all residents to use, and shops and parking on the ground floor. Earlier in the 1930s, Aalto had designed a housing scheme in Finland

ABOVE / THE LONDON COUNTY COUNCIL HOUSING SCHEME IN ROEHAMPTON, LONDON, IS SET IN A MATURE GARDEN SITE RESEMBLING THE "IDEAL GARDEN CITY" DISCUSSED BY LE CORBUSIER MANY YEARS EARLIER.

ABOVE / GOLDFINGER'S BALFRON TOWER WITH ITS ELEVATOR SHAFT ATTACHED TO THE MAIN BUILDING BY WALKWAYS.

that included four high-rise blocks whose fan-shaped plan was similar to that of Neue Vahr. The positioning of the earlier scheme was to be of great importance, as it was with Neue Vahr, so that every resident had views of the sea nearby. However, the Finnish scheme was not built, as the real estate was sold before the building could happen.

Aalto followed a series of principles in his basic housing schemes. He would work with an abstract, nongeometric plan, would always try to include a balcony, terrace, or garden, and would also position the buildings so they were close to nature—water or woodlands.

Many years after his input into the Weissenhof Seidlung exhibition, **Hans Scharoun** built two apartment blocks in the late '50s, also in Stuttgart, called the **Romeo and Juliet.** The Romeo is a nineteen-story block and the Juliet a horseshoe-shaped building that drops from twelve to five stories. Both have penthouse apartments on the top floors. Typical of Scharoun's work, the tall tower is more a compound of flats than an equal breakdown of the block, every floor having no two flats with the same plan or layout. In the Juliet, even though the units are similar to each other, each flat's aspect is completely different. This scheme was a great commercial success, and rather than being developed as a housing association with rental units, each flat was sold outright. The name Romeo and Juliet was selected not because of its symbolism; it came to light during the planning process. The popularity of these blocks led to further commissions in surrounding areas.

ABOVE / THE BARBICAN IN THE CENTER OF LONDON, INITIALLY BUILT FOR CITY WORKERS TO LIVE IN ON A RENTAL BASIS, IS NOW ALMOST COMPLETELY PRIVATELY OWNED. WITH ITS SERVICES, AMENITIES, AND LOCATION, IT IS ONE OF LONDON'S MOST DESIRABLE ADDRESSES.

In the late '50s, **Walter Gropius,** working with The Architect's Collaborative, which he founded, became involved in a massive scheme in the Britz-Buckow-Rudow area of West Berlin. This development, actually commenced many years later, was to house 45,000 people. The Wohnhochhaus Ideal in Gropiusstadt, built in 1969, was one of the buildings from this scheme that was completed.

Harry Seidler, originally from Austria, was educated first in Canada, and then for a short while at Harvard under the guidance of Gropius. Alongside I. M. Pei and Paul Rudolph, Seidler went on to work with Aalto, Breuer, and then Oscar Niemeyer in Brazil, finally settling in Australia in the late 1940s. His Blues Point Tower of the late 1950s, on McMahon's Point, Sydney, now overlooking the Opera House and the Sydney Harbour Bridge, was to be part of a much larger scheme with eight towers and several slab blocks built at different heights so as to protect the harbor views for the entire peninsula at Sydney Harbour. The plan from 1957 had been to develop high-density housing, but unfortunately, the local government did not adopt the idea of the three different heights of housing. Only one block was built. This twenty-four-floor building with its seven units on each floor has spectacular views.

Marina City in Chicago, by **Bertrand Goldberg,** is nicknamed the corncob

When Mies designed his glass tower in the '20s, he knew it was a totally unfeasible project. But forty or so years later construction techniques had evolved to the point where it could be built. **George Schipporeit and John Heinrich,** who had been students of Mies at the Illinois Institute of Technology, went on to work in his office. The abstract, clover-like shape of their building, **Lake Point Tower** of **1968,** does give it a slightly dated feel, but it works well within its setting just on the edge of Lake Michigan. Its bronze framework and glass are highly reflective. Within its seventy floors are some 900 apartments.

In New York, **I. M. Pei and Associates** built **Kips Bay Plaza,** now called Kips

buildings due to its appearance. It was the first U.S. government–funded housing program, and was completed in 1964. Goldberg was at Harvard before Gropius arrived, then went to the Bauhaus from '32 to '33 and worked with Mies van der Rohe. He was influenced by him so much that he believed that all architecture should be Miesian. When he got back to the U.S.A. in 1937, he spent time developing new structural methods and by the '40s had become obsessed with the industrial process and its application to architecture. In the 1950s Goldberg could at last put his industrial experiments to actual use building high-rise towers. In Chicago, his Astor Tower Hotel did have a central core, but the exterior was still of a conventional appearance—a rectilinear form instead of the circular forms he is known for. Soon after this, Marina City was created, built in situ with a rising foundation. At the same time, **Skidmore, Owings and Merrill** were building the monumental **John Hancock Center,** also in Chicago. The endless tapering form of the hundred-story tower of cross braces and smoked glass is visible from wherever you are in Chicago. The lowest forty floors are offices. Above are apartments, observation decks, restaurants, and, of course, the radio facilities high above. Completed in 1970, the John Hancock Center is a building of great geometry. The external cross-bracing acts as support for the whole building and allows tenants and residents enormeous flexibility in designing their homes' internal spaces.

ABOVE / AALTO'S NEUE VAHR HOUSING IN GERMANY HAS A FAN-SHAPED PLAN TO CREATE PRIVACY AND GIVE EVERY RESIDENT A DIFFERENT VIEW. IT ALSO INCLUDES AREAS WHERE NEIGHBORS CAN MEET SOCIALLY.

ABOVE / SCHAROUN'S ROMEO AND JULIET BUILDINGS IN STUTTGART HAVE DIFFERENT PLANS, AND WITHIN EACH, EVERY APARTMENT IS DIFFERENT FROM THE NEXT.

ABOVE / SEIDLER'S BLUES POINT TOWER IN SYDNEY IS ONLY A SINGLE BUILDING OF WHAT WAS TO BE A GREATER SCHEME INCLUDING LOW- AND HIGH-RISE BUILDINGS OF VARIOUS HEIGHTS.

Bay Towers. Located between 30th and 33rd Streets and First and Second Avenues, the twin, slab blocks house over 1000 apartments. This plan has common elements with others in Washington, D.C., Chicago, and Philadelphia by the same firm. The Kips Bay Plaza scheme in Manhattan was part of an urban renewal program. The idea was to find an economic and aesthetic alternative to the usual steel-framed, brick-faced apartment blocks that were expected to be built. I. M. Pei's scheme was for two massive slab blocks of reinforced-concrete poured in situ with a load-bearing facade, which created apartments with fewer internal structural elements and allowed more useable space. The interiors were well lit with floor-to-ceiling windows, but the external grid gave protection from strong sunlight. The one flaw with the whole scheme, however, was the failure to recognize that good design or architecture alone was not enough to replace the previous squalor. Again it was the problem of tenants who were not as progressive as the building they lived in.

In **1967, Paul Rudolph** put together a scheme for a massive mixed project for the Lower Manhattan area of New York, using container-like units stacked up. This would have been the most heavily populated building ever built. This scheme, **Graphic Arts Center,** was to include two skyscraper office blocks, more than four thousand flats on sixty-five floors, a school, a nursery, restaurants, a swimming pool, and mooring for boats in a marina. There were to be a dozen or so floors of workspace for printers and colorists, there were to be traffic-free zones and open plazas. There would have been parking for over 2,000 cars and an enormous utilities space of more than 500,000 square feet. Working with a flexible scheme of capsule-like units, apartments ranging in size from one to six bedrooms could be formed, some with double-height living areas and all with their own roof terraces.

The project sounded like an ideal project for a major city. The living units were to be built by a mobile-home manufacturer. For a while, New Yorkers believed this scheme would really be built. The idea was being packaged and large, color ads were being put in national magazines.

ABOVE / THE JOHN HANCOCK CENTER IN CHICAGO HAS OFFICE AND COMMERCIAL SPACES AT THE LOWER LEVELS AND LIVING ACCOMMODATION AT THE HIGHER LEVELS, WITH OBSERVATION DECKS AND LEISURE FACILITIES THROUGHOUT.

ABOVE / MARINA CITY BY BERTRAND GOLDBERG, NICKNAMED THE CORNCOB BUILDINGS, INCLUDES SHOPS, A HOTEL, PARKING, AND EVEN MOORINGS FOR YOUR BOAT.

ABOVE / SCHIPPOREIT AND HEINRICH'S LAKE POINT TOWER, BASED ON MIES' EARLIER PROJECT FOR A GLASS SKYSCRAPER, HAS A CURVED GLASS EXTERIOR.

One of the many questions asked at the time was, "Who would want to live fifty-two weeks of the year in a caravan, even if it is suspended 600 feet above the world's most breathtaking skyline?" In an interview about this project Rudolph said, "It's been nixed. . . . Architects have to be eternally hopeful people. I never believe anything is going to be built until it is actually in place" ("Storey with an Unhappy Ending," *Daily Telegraph,* London, 1968). But he did believe that the Graphic Arts Center would be built somewhere in the world twenty to twenty-five years later. This was in 1968. Nothing of this size or concept has yet been built.

In 1988, Rudolph went on to use a very similar method of construction for a much, much smaller scheme in Singapore, of all places. The **Colonnade Condominiums** was built for a company called Pontiac Land Private Ltd. with Ove Arup and Partners as engineers, of what appeared to be factory-built housing modules stacked and cantilevered, creating terraces and double-height living rooms.

Peter Cook and Ron Herron were looking to the future with their projects, Plug-in City and Walking City. Both were members of the **Archigram Group,** an organization they formed after working together on the redevelopment of London's Euston Station. Herron's Walking City scheme was a city on the move: it could be located anywhere, could be hooked up to local services, and the residents could direct it to wherever they wanted to go; it would walk to its next location. Cook's Plug-in City, which influenced the design of the Centre Pompidou by Richard Rogers and Renzo Piano ten years later, was to be an ever-changing metropolis. Its intent was to show that people in the future could have a good time living in a new concept of architecture. Cook, Herron, and the other members of the Archigram Group put together a magazine, *Archigram,* and published endless schemes for futuristic projects, one of the best of which was the Archigram Capsule at Osaka's Expo '70.

The housing scheme for Montreal's Expo '67, called **Habitat,** was a prototype solution created by Canadian/Israeli **Moshe Safdie.** It used prefabricated and fitted-out units that were assembled on-site. The irregular, stacked units make up a three-dimensional city which was originally planned to include 1,200 units, shops, schools, and a hotel. For the Expo, only about 150 or so units were created. Habitat was built from 350 concrete boxes, constructed on-site, each 38.5 x 17.5 x 10 feet high, and stacked as a series of steps, up to twelve units high. There were fifteen different configurations of dwellings—some single-level, some double—ranging from one to four bedrooms. The roof of one unit became the garden of the next. There were a few questions asked and a few faults noted at the time of construction. For instance, inherent to the scheme was a lack of privacy; many of the roof terraces and some of the bedroom and living windows were totally visible to neighbors. Also, the economics were unrealistic. Because of the cost it took

ABOVE / KIPPS BAY PLAZA IN NEW YORK CITY WAS PART OF THE MANHATTAN URBAN RENEWAL PROGRAM. EACH OF THE TWO SLAB BLOCKS CONTAINS OVER 1,000 HOUSING UNITS.

to build the Habitat prototype, it became clear that for the original project to clear financially, Safdie would have to create some 2,000 home units in his larger plan if it were ever built. There were also problems with the prefabrication. It took much longer to assemble the units than it did to build them and fit them out, and with so many configurations, every finished unit was different from the next; the kitchen cabinetry, for example, could not be mass-produced.

Twenty-five dwellings were on permanent show for the duration of the Montreal Expo '67, though some of them had a low standard of furnishing. Now Habitat has matured—the landscape has grown in and around the units, softening and giving more privacy to the individual terraces and gardens.

Barcelona-based **Ricardo Bofill,** with his postmodern and classical schemes, was responsible for some of the largest and most original, effective housing projects in the late twentieth century. In Spain and France he built several large-scale developments that incorporated many

historical elements. Sometime after the Second World War, a decision was made by the French local government to build five new towns around Paris. Bofill, at the time, was supported by President Giscard d'Estaing, and was able to put his mark on these new towns. In both Marne-la-Vallée and Saint-Quentin-en-Yvelines, he built many housing estates of monumental scale. "Build Versaille for the people" was a saying that came up at the time. These schemes, with prefabricated concrete panels, were put together like giant jigsaw puzzles. But although the external elements gave an impression of grandeur and classical proportion, on the inside the flats were said to be dreary. It was obvious that more effort had been put into the visual impact of these buildings than into the actual suburban housing issue that was in question; it was the less well-off from Paris who were being put in these suburban developments. So what had originally been conceived of as an ideal living environment soon had all the social problems that existed in other poorly designed environments.

In Tokyo, **Kisho Kurokawa's Nakagin Capsule Tower, 1972,** stands like a stack of boxes waiting to be shipped, similar to Safdie's Habitat and Rudolph's Graphic Arts Center plan for Lower Manhattan. About 140 prefabricated units (or "living capsules"), stacked, slotted, and intersected, were assembled like building blocks and could be put together or taken away as the residents required.

Generally, high-rise building came to a bit of a halt in the '70s: spreading, low-rise developments were being created all over. **Ralph Erskine's Byker Redevelopment** in the north of England, a long, flowing, snake-like complex, though now cherished by its dwellers, was cause for concern from the start because it crowded together in heavy density a large number of people and

ABOVE / A PROJECT BY PAUL RUDOLPH IN ASIA USES A SCHEME SIMILAR TO HIS GRAPHIC ARTS CENTER, WITH PREFABRICATED ELEMENTS ASSEMBLED AND POSITIONED ON-SITE.

ABOVE / PETER COOK AND ARCHIGRAM CREATED PLUG-IN CITY, ONE OF MANY FUTURISTIC PROJECTS DESIGNED BY THIS TEAM, WHO WERE WAY AHEAD OF THEIR TIME.

ABOVE / EXPO '67 HABITAT HOUSING BY MOSHE SAFDIE IN MONTREAL, CREATED A COMPLEX PROJECT OF INTERLOCKING CONCRETE BOXES. THE ROOF OF EACH UNIT CREATES THE TERRACE FOR THE ONE ABOVE IT.

families from problem areas. Erskine set up an office on-site so as to be on call for any problems that might occur. He encouraged local children to come to the office to draw and be involved with local developments.

The high-rise boom had faltered. With social problems erupting from the ghettos some of these schemes created, the fundamental concept of a very high number of people living under one roof had to be rethought. In some parts of the world it worked—to live in a high-rise was prestigious, the place to be. You were proud of your place in the clouds.

It seemed that the concept's failure was because often the wrong people were being put into the high-rises: families with young children, elderly people, and difficult and unsociable individuals were put under one roof and really just forgotten about. In parts of the U.S., similar housing schemes, much larger than anywhere else, caused problems seemingly from the start.

Schemes housing the wrong population still exist; slowly they are being redeveloped. Some are being sold off to individual investors who renovate and sell them for high premiums. In some ways, it is a chance of a lifetime to own a small piece of individual architecture, like buying and owning a limited-edition print or other artwork. The majority of us could not afford a one-of-a-kind house by Mies van der Rohe, but have more of a chance of affording an apartment, like those lucky people in France who live in the Unité d'Habitation.

In the '80s, commercial high-rise carried on, every city getting its mini-Manhattan look. Towers went up, up, and up. Every city's financial area would end up with a group of high-rise buildings. The residential side of architecture was going more toward the reuse of old, unused commercial buildings. Lofts became the place to live. But soon after the loft revolution and the trend toward reusing industrial buildings for residential use, the modern interior became more and more in demand. People started to look for modern buildings to live in.

In Asia, countries were developing so fast that whole cities became building sites. In Hong Kong, the residential high-rise movement went onward and upward. On the hills of Hong Kong, condo after condo went up, perhaps some of them not so architecturally

ABOVE / IN PARIS, LES ARCADES DU LAC, BY BOFILL, BROUGHT POSTMODERN ELEMENTS TO PUBLIC HOUSING. UNFORTUNATELY, THE VISUAL IMPACT OF THE EXTERIOR IS MUCH MORE IMPRESSIVE THAN THE ACTUAL LIVING SPACES.

ABOVE / THE NAKAGIN CAPSULE TOWER IN TOKYO, BY KUROKAWA, FOLLOWS SIMILAR CONCEPTS BY OTHERS OF THE TIME: THE CAPSULES WERE OUTFITTED OFF-SITE AND SLOTTED INTO POSITIONS AT ALL DIFFERENT LEVELS.

important, but at least they were being built. In Hong Kong, the only place to build was up. This is what is starting to happen in the Western world now.

After September 11, 2001, many people thought their building would be the next target, and high-rise living, especially in the United States, was not high on most people's agenda. In the very tall buildings there was a small exodus. The rental market was hit. Now we have come to terms with this, however, and throughout the world the high-rise boom is back.

New towers are going up in cities the world over, many of which are multipurposed: you can live and work in the same place, go to the rooftop restaurant to entertain, and park your car on the thirtieth floor. Despite the very modern, twenty-first-century feel of this setup, it all goes back to the mid-twentieth century, and perhaps before, when these were only ideas on paper and that was as far as it went.

ABOVE / ERSKINE'S BYKER HOUSING CONSISTS OF A CONTINUOUS SNAKE-LIKE BLOCK SET AMONGST VARIOUS OTHER HOUSING UNITS.

ABOVE / CANARY WHARF WAS THE START OF THE NEW WAVE OF HIGH-RISE BUILDING IN LONDON'S DOCKLANDS AREA. NOW MORE AND MORE TOWERS, A MIX OF BOTH RESIDENTIAL AND COMMERCIAL, ARE BEING BUILT.

ABOVE / THE HONG KONG SKYLINE IS FULL OF HIGH-RISE RESIDENTIAL BLOCKS. IN HONG KONG, THE BUILDING TREND HAS BEEN FOLLOWING THIS DIRECTION, "UP," FOR MANY YEARS. MANY OTHER CITIES ARE BEGINNING TO DEVELOP THIS WAY NOW TOO.

CHRONOLOGY

1881, Monadnock Building, Chicago, Daniel H. Burnham and J. W. Root

1890, Wainwright Building, St. Louis, Missouri, Louis Sullivan and Dankmar Adler

1899, Carson Pirie & Scott Department Store, Chicago, Louis Sullivan

1902, Flatiron Building, New York City, Daniel H. Burnham

1902, Apartments rue Franklin, Paris, Auguste Perret

1913, Woolworth Building, New York City, Cass Gilbert

1925, Bauhaus Buildings, Dessau, Germany, Walter Gropius

1928, Project for St. Marks in the Bouwerie, New York City, Frank Lloyd Wright

1929, Siemenstadt project, near Berlin, Walter Gropius, Hans Scharoun

1930, Chrysler Building, New York City, William Van Alen

1931, Empire State Building, New York City, Shreve, Lamb and Harmon

1933, Highpoint I, London, Berthold Lubetkin

1933, Paimio Sanatorium, Paimio, Finland, Alvar Aalto

1934, Isokon Flats, London, Wells Coates

1935, Embassy Court, Brighton, U.K., Wells Coates

1938, Highpoint II, London, Berthold Lubetkin

1940, Rockefeller Center, New York City, Hood, Hofmeister, Reinhard, Corbett, Harrison, MacMurray, Godley, and Fouilhoux

1943, Ministry of Education and Health, Costa Rio, Brazil, Le Corbusier, Oscar Niemeyer

1944, Johnson Wax Research Tower, Racine, Wisconsin, Frank Lloyd Wright

1946, Unité d'Habitation, Marseille, France, Le Corbusier

1946, Promontory Apartments, Chicago, Ludvig Mies van der Rohe

1951, Lake Shore Drive Apartments, Chicago, Ludvig Mies van der Rohe

1952, Mill Creek I, Philadelphia, Louis I. Kahn

1952, Lever Building, New York City, Skidmore, Owings and Merrill

1953, Price Tower, Bartlesville, Oklahoma, Frank Lloyd Wright

1955, Roehampton Housing Estate, London, London County Council

1956, Lake Meadows Apartments, Chicago, Skidmore, Owings and Merrill

1956, Golden Lane Estate, London, Chamberlin, Powell and Bon

1956, 910 Lake Shore Drive, Chicago, Ludvig Mies van der Rohe

1957, Blues Point Tower, Sydney, Harry Seidler

1958, Neue Vahr, Bremen Germany, Alvar Aalto

1958, Seagram Building, New York City, Mies van der Rohe with Phillip Johnson

1959, Barbican, London, Chamberlin, Powell and Bon

1959, Pirelli Tower, Milan, Gio Ponti

1959, Romeo and Juliet Buildings, Stuttgart Germany, Hans Scharoun

1960, Cluster Blocks, London, Denys Lasdun

1963, Kips Bay Plaza, New York City, I. M. Pei

1963, PanAm Building, New York City, Walter Gropius and Pietro Belluschi

1964, Post Office Tower, London, Eric Bedford

1964, Balfron Tower, London, Erno Goldfinger

1966, Centrepoint, London, Richard Seifert

1967, Graphic Arts Center, New York City, Paul Rudolph

1967, Expo '67 Habitat, Montreal, Moshe Safdie

1968, John Hancock Center, Chicago, Skidmore, Owings and Merrill

1970, Byker Redevelopment, Newcastle, U.K., Ralph Erskine

1972, Nakagin Capsule Tower, Tokyo, Kisho Kurokawa

1972, World Trade Center, New York City, Minoru Yamasaki

1974, Les Arcades du Lac, Paris, Ricardo Bofill

1976, Sony Tower, Tokyo, Kisho Kurokawa

1978, Les Espaces d'Abraxas, Paris, Ricardo Bofill

1980, Colonnade Condominiums, Singapore, Paul Rudolph

1980, NatWest Bank Building, London, Richard Seifert

1982, AT&T Building, New York City, Johnson/Burgee

1986, Shanghai and Bangkok Bank, Hong Kong, Norman Foster

1991, Canary Wharf, London, Cesar Pelli

1997, Petronas Towers, Kuala Lumpur, Malaysia, Cesar Pelli

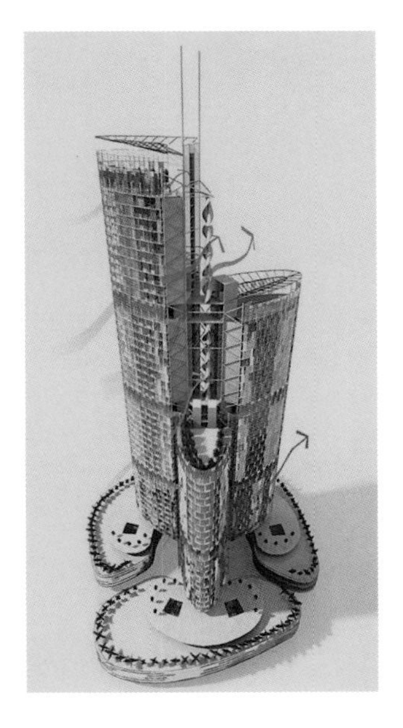

ABOVE / THE FUTURE'S NEW CITY: THIS ONE IS PROPOSED FOR A SITE IN LONDON, AND IS TYPICAL OF A FUTURE CITY-WITHIN-A-CITY. EACH TOWER WILL INCLUDE ALL YOU NEED FOR LIVING, WORKING, AND PLAYING.

CLASSIC HIGH-RISE

The word "classic" sums up the **feeling of timelessness** encompassed in the high-rises in this section. Here, these high-rise buildings will be showcased either as they were when first built or in new photography as restored or renovated units that have **stood the test of time. They stand out from the rest.**

A cross section of archive material and new images shows these **great classics to their best advantage,** from Frank Lloyd Wright's early project for the Price Tower in Oklahoma (very recently transformed into a boutique hotel) to an underrated scheme for retirement in Florida by Sarasota School of Architecture architect Frank Folsom Smith.

This section will show a variety of residences in various locations—**in the city, in a rambling green park, and on the water.**

The buildings here are classics of their time. Nothing has exceeded them in what they do. One may have an amazing elevation, while another may be placed in such an ideal setting that it's the views that make it what it is.

THE BARBICAN, LONDON

This rambling complex in the city of London by Chamberlin, Powell and Bon was initially conceived in 1955. It was finished in the late 1970s as a complete city-within-a-city. It was commissioned by the local authorities for affordable housing.

The Barbican was built of in situ concrete that was poured on-site in molds with granite aggregate, to retain uniformity in character and to withstand weather extremes. The complex consists of more than 2,000 units ranging from houses, low-rises, duplexes, and large high-rise apartments with terraces. The three towers, each well over forty floors, hold three apartments on each level, and a penthouse on the top. The sumptuous penthouse apartments each have three levels themselves; on the first level are the living, dining, and kitchen areas, a balcony, and a bedroom with a shower room. On the middle level are three bedrooms (one en suite), a dressing room, and a gallery above the living area, giving a double-height room. On the top level is a large conservatory and room terrace. All this at about thirty floors up.

The Barbican development includes a theatre, concert hall, cinema, art gallery, library, various restaurants, sports facilities, a pool with landscaping and wildlife, both indoor and outdoor landscape gardens, and ample underground parking and storage.

The high-rise residential towers, triangular in plan, house the largest apartments in the complex, all with balconies capturing great views of London and the surrounding areas. It was thought at the time they were built that the apartments in the towers were the least desirable, with a single aspect and all the rooms leading off a long corridor. Now, however, they are the most desirable. New owners are remodeling them and opening up the layout to create larger living areas for today's way of life.

In the crush of applications from families with children, the original intent of the Barbican's wide range of accommodations—to house mainly people from middle- to upper-income brackets who would probably leave on weekends for their country home and probably not have many children—was forgotten.

Over the years, the city of London sold off these flats and now the majority of the units are privately owned. The whole complex is now protected and there are many sources of information for the restoration and reinstatement of the apartments.

LEFT PAGE / A VIEW AT TIME OF THE BARBICAN'S CONSTRUCTION, FROM THE TOP OF ONE OF ITS TOWERS, SHOWS THE MIX OF LOW- AND HIGH-LEVEL HOUSING THAT WAS GOING UP AROUND IT.

ABOVE LEFT / THE ORIGINAL KITCHEN, STILL INTACT IN MANY APARTMENTS, WAS DESIGNED SPECIALLY FOR THIS COMPLEX. THE CABINETS RESEMBLE THE CABINETS ON A YACHT.

ABOVE / IN ONE OF THE LOW-RISE UNITS, VARIOUS LEVELS DIVIDE THE SPACE INTO ITS DIFFERENT USES.

RIGHT PAGE / BATHROOMS WERE COMPLETELY TILED, AND HOUSED SIMPLE CABINETS. AT THAT TIME, IT COULDN'T GET MUCH MORE MODERN.

BLUES POINT TOWER, SYDNEY

Harry Seidler's Blues Point Tower, built on what is now protected parkland, is a very small part of a greater scheme planned in the 1950s. Perhaps if the whole development had gone ahead it might not have been so successful, and that would be another story.

On this prime site the view is one of the most noted features. Built from a slab-and-cross-wall system, the building was built in situ from continuous-poured concrete that included the stairwells and elevator shaft. An off-white brick fills in the reinforced-concrete framework.

Completed in 1961, the block of some twenty-four floors includes shops on the ground level, a laundry and drying yard near the top of the building, and an observation deck at the top. The 168 apartments, divided seven to a floor, are laid out in one of three alternating floor plans: four two-bedroom corner flats, one one-bed flat, and two studio flats.

The corner flats have French balconies—full-height, glazed sliding doors that open onto a narrow open recess. There are sliding aluminum windows in the bedrooms too, placed in strip formation. The air ducts control the positioning of the kitchens and bathrooms, keeping all the communal pipework to a minimum.

The elevations reflect the alternate apartment floor plans in which the staggered effect of the corner balconies not only gives different views, but also satisfies fire regulations with a solid masonry wall between each glazed opening.

At present the building is still alone in its landscape of greenery, a great location and landmark of Sydney's skyline.

LEFT PAGE / BLUES POINT TOWER SITS IN FRONT OF THE SYDNEY HARBOUR BRIDGE LIKE A GEM IN A GIANT STEEL RING. THIS TOWER WAS TO BE ONE OF MANY RESIDENTIAL TOWERS BUILT ON THIS SITE.

NEXT PAGE / A TYPICAL APARTMENT WITH A FRENCH BALCONY AND OPEN-PLAN LAYOUT. CLASSIC PIECES OF MIDCENTURY MODERN FURNITURE—THE BERTOIA DIAMOND CHAIRS AND THE FLORENCE KNOLL SOFA—HAVE A TIMELESS LOOK.

UNITÉ D'HABITATION, MARSEILLE

Le Corbusier's Unité d'Habitation, in his words a "vertical garden city," is an apartment block with its own shopping street halfway up the building. It also includes a hotel, a school on the roof, barber shops, a café, and every other necessary service for day-to-day living, all set in gardens and raised above the ground on massive concrete columns, or *pilotis*.

One of the first proposals for the Marseille project was for three buildings to be placed at right angles to each other, spaced adequately apart so as not to overlook each other.

The original plan called for one small block and two larger ones. It was the plan for the larger blocks that became the version we today know as the Unité d'Habitation.

Le Corbusier was invited to design this building to house 1,500 people just after World War II. He accepted the commission on the condition that all building regulations and controls could be allowed to be ignored. Finding that regular machine-made materials—such as steel, the basis of new architecture—had become very expensive, and being given the green light he had so long been waiting for on the scheme, Le Corbusier had to come up with a feasible solution.

He had used concrete in his earlier houses, but always only as a base material coated with plaster, smoothed off, and painted. This building would be different. He abandoned the idea of trying ways to finish off the concrete with a smooth surface. Instead, it would be poured into molds made of rough wooden boards in situ, which would leave an impression in the concrete, thus creating a pattern. What emerged was a material of great masculine properties, a product that was reasonably economic, and a method that did not require great skill to apply.

The building was raised on massive *pilotis* floats above the ground. The elevation of the building is broken up into individual units, the balconies enclosed with precast, pierced low walls. The flank walls of each terrace are painted a different color.

To some, the impact of the massive concrete block can be off-putting, but once you note the detailing, the shuttering technique, and the important use of color, it becomes more approachable and inviting. The more you look at the building, the more you experience the total concept.

LEFT PAGE / THE EXTERIOR OF THE BUILDING SHOWS THE POURED-CONCRETE FINISH AND DETAILING THROUGHOUT. THE USE OF COLOR HIGHLIGHTS THE FLANK WALLS OF THE TERRACES.

ABOVE / THE MAIN LIVING AREA OPENS ONTO A SCREENED, CONCRETE TERRACE. THE TWO-STORY APARTMENT, THOUGH QUITE SMALL, FEELS SPACIOUS WITH SO MUCH LIGHT STREAMING THROUGH.

ABOVE / ONE OF THE UNITÉ D'HABITATION'S NARROW BEDROOMS. THERE IS A FULL-HEIGHT SLIDING PARTITION BETWEEN THE NEIGHBORING ROOMS.

PRICE TOWER, BARTLESVILLE, OKLAHOMA

Frank Lloyd Wright's Price Tower was inspired by his design for a tower in New York that was never built, St Mark's in the Bouwerie, 1929. The Price Tower, commissioned by Harold Price, was to be a 221-foot tower for both office and residential use. In the '20s, Price was a small-time welder when he first met Wright, who throughout his life built several buildings for the Price family. Price ended up owning one of the largest pipeline construction companies in the U.S.A.

The Price Tower, like the earlier St Mark's, was to be constructed with a taproot—a very deep central core foundation—that allowed for cantilevered floors from, in this case, the four steel-and-reinforced-concrete cores which also acted as elevator shafts. The cantilevered floors meant that the exterior walls would not be load-bearing and so could be almost completely of glass. This method allowed for much more lightweight materials to be used in construction, with the end result that buildings were cheaper to build and, eventually, could be much taller.

Wright had proposed this building method back in the 1920s, but it took some thirty years for him to use it himself. Many other architects, in the meantime, had been developing the idea further and successfully using it.

This tower and the S. C. Johnson Wax Research Building of 1945 were the only two Frank Lloyd Wright ideas for high-rise buildings to be realized. The Price Tower is now on the National Register of Historic Buildings.

With this tower, Wright fulfilled his ideas of a multiuse skyscraper: a tall, elegant, detailed building that united the workplace and the place to live.

In the Price Tower, only part of each floor was to be residential. The building is in four quadrants, with the apartments being double-height units on the southwest corner of the building. They have small balconies that protrude from the exterior curtain-wall of glass, marking the location of the bedrooms. The exterior of the building is clad in copper panels—now green with patina—which, besides being decorative, act as sunshades, being vertical on the apartment sides of the building and horizontal on the office sides. On the top floor are rooftop gardens that make the building an idyllic environment in which to live, work, and play.

Now the building houses the Price Tower Arts Center and on the top floors you can stay at the Inn at Price Tower, a bed-and-breakfast hotel.

LEFT PAGE / THE DOUBLE-HEIGHT RESIDENTIAL UNITS ARE VISIBLE FROM THE EXTERIOR ELEVATIONS. THE SMALL, TRIANGULAR BALCONIES GIVE AWAY WHERE THE BEDROOMS ARE.

ABOVE / F. W. PRICE'S OFFICE IN THE TOWER INCLUDES THIS MOSAIC FEATURE IN GLASS AND METAL. IT REPEATS THE TRIANGULAR MOTIF SEEN IN OTHER ELEMENTS THROUGHOUT THE BUILDING.

ABOVE / IN THE LOWER FLOOR OF THE DOUBLE-HEIGHT UNITS, THE DECORATION AND DETAILING HAS ALL BEEN FINISHED TO FRANK LLOYD WRIGHT'S ORIGINAL DESIGN. THE MURAL IS PAINTED.

ABOVE / THE TOWER'S ENTRANCE LOBBY INTRODUCES THE THEME OF THE TRIANGLE AS A DECORATIVE ELEMENT.

ABOVE / THE SHAPE OF A TRIANGULARLY PLANNED KITCHEN IS REFLECTED, AMONG OTHER PLACES, IN THE LIGHTING UNITS.

PLYMOUTH HARBOR, SARASOTA, FLORIDA

The initial concept for Plymouth Harbor was announced early one winter morning. Dr. John Whitney MacNeil, senior minister of the First Congregational Church of Sarasota, Florida, woke his wife at 4 a.m. and said, "I simply must tell you now, our church is going to build a retirement home of distinction."

"Yes dear, go back to sleep," she murmured.

MacNeil was concerned about the way older people moving to Sarasota were often away from their family and friends. He wanted them to live out their, in many cases, long last years fully, have consistent care, have the opportunity to be involved in hobbies and interests, and be part of a community.

After his early-morning vision he called the national church officials and started putting his plans into action. Despite the fifty-dollar contribution from each of the five members on the board of trustees, serious financial support had to be found. Homer Myers, a Sarasota banker who was on the board of trustees from early days, was so inspired by MacNeil's vision that he lent him the money.

There were, of course, many other issues to sort out. Finding the site was the first critical problem. Coon Key, a seventeen-acre lot with mangroves, sparkling water, wildlife, and amazing, clear views of the local area, was the selected site. Architect Frank Folsom Smith started his own practice with this building, the largest job ever commissioned to a local. Working with Louis Schneider, he had many other problems to solve: the thirty-five foot height limit, the flood hazard, and protests from local residents concerned about preserving the environment.

The zoning, which prohibited anything from being built over thirty-five feet high, had to be changed; it would have been much more damaging to the surrounding area to do what the law allowed than what it didn't. How this happened is unclear; as Frank Smith says, "We could have dredged and created a landfill," but he was determined that he would not fill in the bay.

So the twenty-five story building was designed. Built at the rate of one floor a week, the whole building was complete in about sixteen months. Initially there were 340 apartments, but because of the forward-thinking planning of the architects, there are now about 220: each apartment was conceived with flexibility and walls were not load-bearing, so they could be repositioned or removed to make bigger or smaller units.

The idea behind Plymouth Harbor was that it be different from any other retirement housing. MacNeil visited endless retirement homes before the final plans were decided upon. It was not to be like an institution, and it was not to have endless corridors. He wanted it to be broken up into communities and neighborhoods.

So, for every three floors a communal area was created—an interior three-story open space is used for meetings, games, chatting, and entertaining. Also, each area has a communal kitchen and outdoor space. These neighborhoods are called colonies and each elects a representative to attend general meetings relating to the whole building and community.

Completed in 1966, this concrete building with balconies on all sides was the first high-rise building in Sarasota, and is a landmark visible from great distances.

In 1991 Plymouth Harbor won a coveted "Test of Time" award from the Florida Institute of Architects. It was praised for its sensitive relationship to its site, its striking exterior, and its innovative concept of interior colonies. Unfortunately, the scheme has never been repeated, probably because of the high cost of real estate in that region.

This adult-living high-rise facility has a five-year waiting list for future residents. It shows how good design, well-conceived ideas, and good management can make high-density accommodation in high-rise buildings work well.

LEFT PAGE / LOOKING ACROSS THE BAYOU AT PLYMOUTH HARBOR, ONE CAN SEE THE FLOORS WITH THE OPEN TERRACES, GIVING AWAY THE LOCATION OF THE COLONY LEVELS.

ABOVE / PLYMOUTH HARBOR, ONE OF SARASOTA'S TALLEST BUILDINGS, IS IN AN IDYLLIC SETTING. TO THE LEFT IS THE BAYOU.

RIGHT PAGE / THE INTERIOR THREE-STORY COMMON SPACE, FOUND AT REGULAR INTERVALS THROUGHOUT THE BUILDING, CREATES A NEIGHBORHOOD. NEIGHBORHOODS ARE CALLED COLONIES.

HIGHPOINT II, LONDON

Built in 1937 as a companion to the slightly earlier Highpoint I in North London, this Berthold Lubetkin masterpiece was the highest residence in London when it was built. The architect lived for sixteen years in Highpoint II's penthouse, which he designed for himself.

The contractor who commissioned Highpoint I bought the adjacent plot to end the risk of something unsympathetic being built next door. The authorities did not want another modern building to go up. Lubetkin got around this by pulling the wool over the authorities' eyes and showing a series of conventional designs with historical references. Because of the building's complexity, it took over a year to get the project through the design process.

Highpoint II, set alongside the reinforced-concrete monolith of Highpoint I, is softer because of the mixture of materials used on its exterior: brick infill, tiled panels, and less-regular balconies. In this "ideal garden city" these two buildings were as close as you could get to, in Le Corbusier's words, the "vertical garden city," with its surrounding landscape, communal areas, and many facilities.

In Highpoint II there are two types of flats: "one with maximum number of rooms for the use of large families, and the other with the number of rooms sacrificed to the size and importance of the main living room. The latter type, occupying the center block, is on the duplex principle, each flat having two floors connected by an internal staircase but with the large living room rising the full height. This provides a central reception space with imposing scale taking full advantage of the view over the garden to Hampstead Heath. This view is framed in a window sixteen feet high by ten feet wide. The wings either side of this central block are occupied by maisonette flats, also with an internal staircase" (*Architectural Record,* October 1938).

Lubetkin's penthouse on the roof, a late addition to the building design, filled his need for having somewhere his friends and visitors could see his two buildings from the best advantage and view London from above and at a distance.

In the '90s, the penthouse was sold to furniture designer Ou Baholyodhin and painter Erez Yardini. They knew as soon as they moved in that they had to restore it to its original state. They called John Allan of Avanti Architects, the author of several books on Lubetkin, to help with the restoration. Because it is on the roof, the space has a unique layout: a large central room with vaulted ceilings and windows on both sides. A sliding wall of glass opens up the room to the outside space, a full-length terrace. The materials used on the interior, like those used on the exterior, are a mixture of types, from scorched-pine wall boards to gridded quarry tile floors.

The new owners have been so meticulous about the restoration that they have had some of the original furniture, designed by Lubetkin for this apartment, reinstalled.

LEFT PAGE / HIGHPOINT II IS DOMINATED BY THE WHITE MONOLITH, HIGHPOINT I, IN FRONT OF IT. COMMUNAL GARDENS AND TENNIS COURTS UNITE THE TWO BUILDINGS.

ABOVE (TOP) / THIS APARTMENT'S INTERIOR HAS BEEN METICULOUSLY RESTORED BY ITS PRESENT OWNERS. WITH WINDOWS ON BOTH SIDES, THE LIVING SPACE IS BRIGHT AND WELCOMING.

ABOVE (BOTTOM) / A GREAT MIXTURE OF MATERIALS HAS BEEN USED TO DECORATE THROUGHOUT, FROM THE QUARRY TILE FLOORS, THE TRAVERTINE SHELF, AND THE SCORCHED-PINE WALL BOARDS, TO THE COWHIDE OF THE LUBETKIN-DESIGNED FURNITURE. THE COMBINATION WORKS TOGETHER TO CREATE A LUXURIOUS UNITY.

RIGHT PAGE / THE BEDROOM HAS ACCESS TO THE TERRACE, WHERE THE QUARRY TILE GRID FOLLOWS THROUGH. AN EAMES "LA CHAISE" BALANCES THE CURVE OF THE WALL BEHIND IT.

NAKAGIN CAPSULE TOWER, TOKYO

The Nakagin Capsule Tower, built in 1970 in central Tokyo, was from the beginning a concept by Kisho Kurokawa for actual use. Although many architects had come up with projects to be built from prefabricated units and assembled on-site, before the Nakagin Capsule Tower, none of them had ever been realized.

This prefabricated building of between eleven and thirteen stories on each side completes a scheme of 140 units.

The concept behind the project was to create a residential habitat in the center of the city for commuters from out of town to live in during the week. Each unit was mass-produced, hoisted by crane, and assembled into position on a central core with a high-tension bolt system. The architectural design allowed for possibilities of visual change as capsules were added or removed.

As Kurokawa put it, "This is a symbiosis between material and spirit. The concept also expresses the aesthetic of metabolism, the aesthetic of transience."

Each unit was completely furnished with appliances and electrical systems, from audio to telephone. The whole interior was assembled off-site, prior to positioning on the core, and transported to its final destination as a complete interior with fabric-covered walls and carpeted floors. The capsules of reinforced concrete were placed in various layouts on each level of the tower. With a large circular porthole window as the only source of natural light, the interiors were very futuristic with completely built-in storage units, a pull-down desk, an airplane-like bathroom—everything made especially for its use in this building.

Relating somewhat to Moshe Safdie's Habitat, the futuristic work of the Archigram office, and the ideas of Paul Rudolph, the Nakagin Capsule Tower proves that mass production, done well, does work.

LEFT PAGE / STACKED UP, THESE UNITS LOOK LIKE CONTAINERS WAITING TO BE SHIPPED.

TOP LEFT / PREFABRICATED UNITS CAN BE SLOTTED INTO VARIOUS POSITIONS AROUND A CENTRAL CORE. THE CIRCULAR WINDOWS HAVE FAN-LIKE TREATMENTS.

BOTTOM LEFT / DESIGNED FOR SPACE EFFICIENCY, THE BUILT-IN EVERYTHING OF NAKAGIN'S KITCHEN AND BATHROOM UNITS ARE NONETHELESS ATTRACTIVE.

TOP RIGHT / THE COMPACT, PREFORMED BATHROOM UNIT, ULTRA-MODERN AND ULTRA-EFFICIENT.

BOTTOM RIGHT / THERE IS COMMUNAL AREA ON THE FIRST FLOOR WHERE RESIDENTS CAN SOCIALIZE IN GROUPS LARGER THAN THE TWO OR THREE PEOPLE WHO WILL FIT INTO EACH APARTMENT.

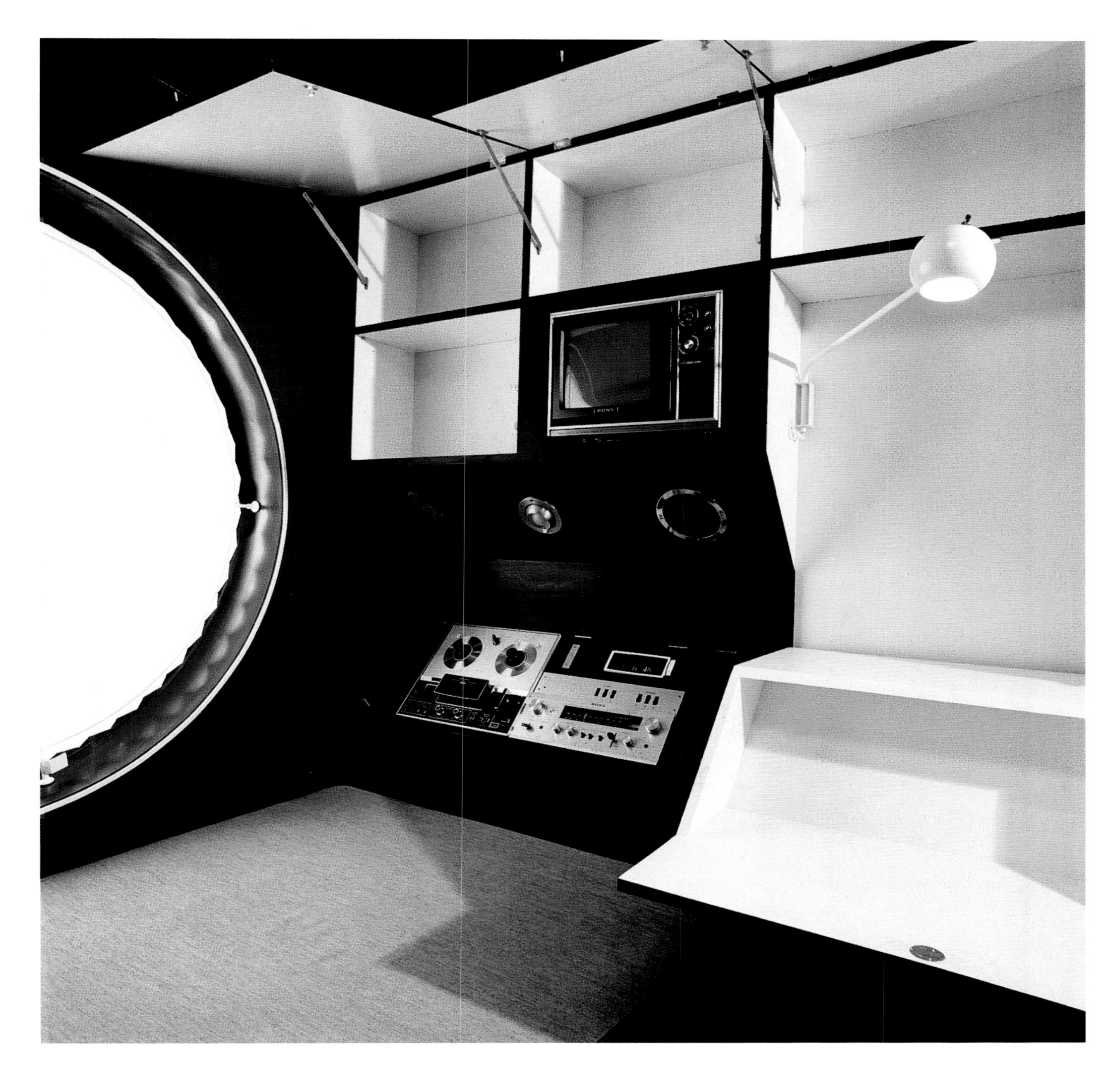

ABOVE / AN INTERIOR VIEW OF A TYPICAL UNIT SHOWING ITS BUILT-IN CABINETRY WITH TV AND STEREO.

MARINA CITY, CHICAGO

Bertrand Goldberg's Marina City, built in 1959, was a $36 million project built in the center of Chicago's Loop on a lot of only about three acres.

The two sixty-floor towers have apartments on the top forty floors and a twenty-story parking lot below. At this building, "the city within a city," you can park your car, moor your boat, go to the theatre, shop, enjoy sports activities, and spend time in the sculpture gardens at ground level as well as enjoy the magnificent views of the city—and all of this on the Chicago River.

There were originally about 450 apartments, though at present there are fewer as some have been knocked together to make larger spaces. As built, the apartments are quite compact, each with one bedroom, one bathroom, a kitchen, and a roomy living/dining room. In addition, all apartments have terraces off both their living and sleeping areas.

These towers, nicknamed "the corncobs" due to their similarity to the vegetable in appearance, are constructed with a concrete, thirty-five-foot-diameter, cylindrical core that houses the utilities. This construction method also created a rising foundation for the cranes and other construction vehicles to work from.

This building was Goldberg's reaction to the need for urban development. He predicted that its design concepts would continue to predominate building construction for the next forty years.

He was right. When you visit Marina City there is nothing you could do to the apartments to make them more modern.

Larry Converso, Chicago-based midcentury modern furniture and design dealer, has lived here for a while now. He has restored his apartment to the original, while subtly bringing it right up to date with a simple, complementary interior. Every surface is white, and almost every piece of furniture is white or glass and metal. This decorating arrangement enables the building's structural details to be in the foreground of each room. The arched beams, wedge-shaped rooms, semicircular terraces, and original fittings make this space a complete, preserved example of Goldberg's vision "to create a new aesthetic experience."

LEFT PAGE / LOOKING UP AT THE TWO TOWERS ONE CAN SEE THE INTEGRAL CAR-PARKING AREAS AT THE LOWER LEVELS.

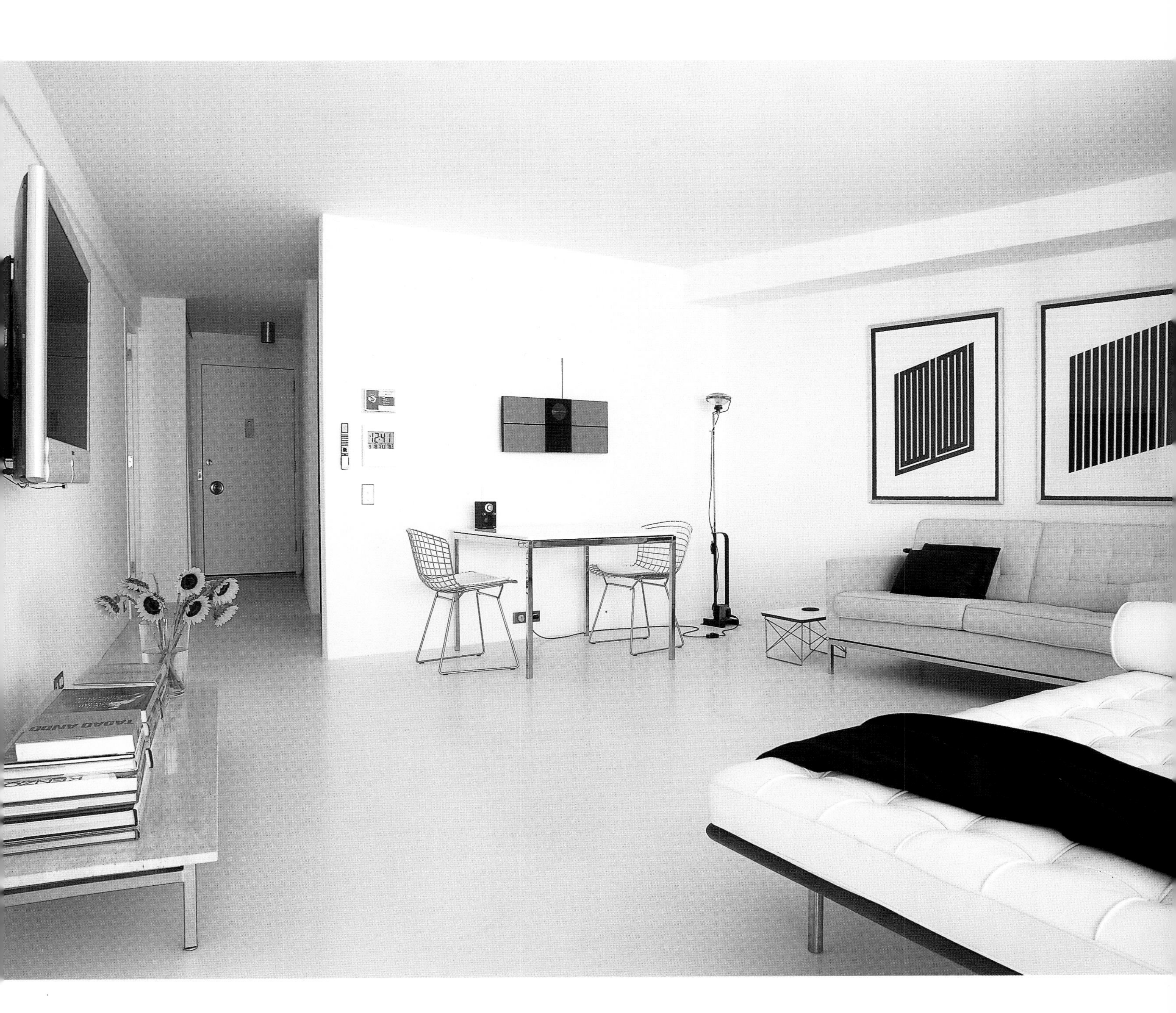

ABOVE / LOOKING TOWARD THE ENTRANCE DOOR FROM THE LIVING ROOM, THE CLEAN PLANE OF THE FLOOR, WHITE VINYL SQUARES THROUGHOUT, BECOMES ANOTHER DECORATIVE SURFACE.

LEFT PAGE / A COMPLETELY WHITE INTERIOR IS GIVEN DEPTH AND TEXTURE WITH A SOFA BY FLORENCE KNOLL AND DAYBED BY MIES VAN DER ROHE.

ABOVE / THE CABINETS OUTSIDE THE BATHROOM, ALL ORIGINAL, KEEP YOU WELL ORGANIZED.

RIGHT / THE SEMICIRCULAR TERRACE GIVES A WIDE VIEW ACROSS THE URBAN LANDSCAPE OF CHICAGO. THE OUTDOOR FURNITURE IS BY RICHARD SHULTZ.

GRAND PLAZA
APARTMENTS
312-64-GRAND
NOW LEASING

COMMONWEALTH PLAZA, CHICAGO

Designed for Herbert Greenwald, the property developer who wanted, according to Mies van der Rohe, "to leave his stamp on the scene" by building the best architecture possible in consideration of modern techniques and economies, this two-story apartment raised over the top of one of the Commonwealth Plaza buildings overlooking Lincoln Park, is a unique piece of Miesian architecture. Hidden away and set back from the main facade of the building, the structure is not visible from the street until you are on the far side of the park.

Commonwealth Plaza, 310 Diversey Street, similar to 860 and 880 Lake Shore Drive but built five or so years later, has silver aluminum coatings and I beams, whereas the earlier buildings have a black steel finish. This makes Commonwealth Plaza appear to be much lighter, fresher, and perhaps more modern.

The Mies van der Rohe/Greenwald relationship came to an abrupt end when Greenwald was killed in 1959 in an airplane crash. His widow continued to live in the penthouse until the mid '70s, when it was purchased by a young family who, in their expansion, moved away from the Miesian ideals, completely covering the marble floors and creating more bedrooms. Luckily, some of the major features were left alone: the glass mosaic bathrooms with floating cabinets, the marble and aluminum staircase, and beneath the carpet, the completely marble floors spreading from inside to out. The present owners moved in in 1990. They called in architects from Powell/Kleinschmidt Inc., whose modernist and minimalist design principles led them to restore the house to its former simplicity.

Because the penthouse is raised off the roof, you cannot see the edge of the main building from the inside. Looking out, you feel as though the marble floor just flows through the floor-to-ceiling windows out to the lake, and into the park looking across to downtown Chicago. With windows on three sides, this residence must have the best views in the city.

In the restoration, Powell/Kleinschmidt Inc. worked closely with the Chicago Historical Society to obtain original plans to ensure correct reinstatements were made. They even called upon Greenwald's widow for advice on certain things. Some elements had to be updated, however, and while trying not to alter any of Mies' proportions, they made built-in closets and cabinets and installed new lighting at the ceiling's edge so as not to interfere with the intended clean, flat, unadorned plane.

Now, of course, the furniture is arranged as a composition in space, with Barcelona chairs, classic sofas and collected objects. This penthouse is still unknown to some of the building's other residents, its entrance is so discreet. Through an exit door and up to an unmarked door, it remains a well-kept secret.

LEFT PAGE / TWO BUILDINGS MAKE UP THIS DEVELOPMENT. THE GRAY, ALUMINUM EXTERIOR GIVES A LIGHTER APPEARANCE TO THE MASSIVE BLOCKS, PARTICULARLY WHEN COMPARED TO THE LAKE SHORE DRIVE APARTMENT BUILDINGS.

TOP LEFT / THE FURNITURE HAS BEEN PLACED DELIBERATELY, AS A COMPOSITION IN SPACE, IN MIESIAN MANNER. THE STAIRCASE—AN ALUMINUM FRAME WITH MARBLE TREADS—IS A UNIQUE PIECE OF MIES VAN DER ROHE DESIGN. THE ENTIRE SPACE IS SURROUNDED WITH FULL-HEIGHT WINDOWS.

BOTTOM LEFT / THE SECOND-FLOOR LANDING CONTINUES THE SAME MARBLE FINISHING AS THE FLOORS BELOW. THE DETAILING IS ALL ORIGINAL, TO MIES' SPECIFICATION.

LEFT PAGE / THE TERRACE OF THE APARTMENT ON THE ROOF OF THE MIES PENTHOUSE AT COMMONWEALTH PLAZA. THE MARBLE CONTINUES INSIDE.

TOP RIGHT / THE HALF-LANDING LOOKS ONTO THE WRAPAROUND TERRACE AND BEYOND, TO DOWNTOWN CHICAGO.

BOTTOM RIGHT / EVEN THE BATHROOM HAS A VIEW IN THIS APARTMENT. THE VANITY UNIT APPEARS TO FLOAT BETWEEN THE TILED WALLS. THE CABINET, WHICH ALSO APPEARS TO BE FLOATING, IS SUSPENDED IN FRONT OF THE WINDOW.

ABOVE / AS THE MIES PENTHOUSE IS ONE OF THE HIGHEST RESIDENTIAL UNITS AROUND, THE PANORAMIC VIEWS ARE BREATHTAKING.

LAKE SHORE DRIVE APARTMENTS, CHICAGO

The apartments at 860 and 880 Lake Shore Drive are perhaps the most famous residential buildings in the world. Every book you pick up about twentieth-century architecture will include a photograph of these buildings.

It was in the late 1940s that construction on the project started. This scheme was a further development of Mies van der Rohe's earlier Promontory Apartments, also in Chicago, and the fulfillment of the glass-tower ideas he had designed in the 1920s. The buildings have steel skeletons and window elements that fit into the framework. The construction was based on a series of bays, five on the building's long sides and three on the others. Each bay was divided into four windows. On the exterior of the building, the concrete-covered skeleton was finished with black steel. Eight-inch I beams were then welded onto this to create a sense of height and upwardness. The use of the I beam as decoration was questioned by many. Mies replied he had two reasons for its use:

> It was very important to preserve and extend the rhythm which the mullions set up on the rest of the building. We looked at it on the model without the steel section attached to the corner column and it did not look right. That is the real reason.
>
> Now, the other reason is that this steel section was needed to stiffen the plate which covers the corner column so this plate would not ripple, and also we needed it for strength when the sections were hoisted into place. Now, of course, that's a very good reason, but the other reason is the real reason!

These buildings at 860 and 880 Lake Shore Drive were the prototypes of many future high-rise developments.

This apartment on the twenty-sixth floor, owned by architect Michael Pado and his wife, art dealer Alice Adams, was remodeled more than twenty years ago. The remodeling included adding part of the neighboring apartment to enlarge the space. They have lived in the building for about thirty years.

Their corner apartment has views across Lake Michigan, from Navy Pier on the southeast to the Indiana Dunes National Lakeshore on the other side of the lake.

The apartment has travertine floors throughout, replicating the entrance lobby to the building. The positioning of the furniture follows Mies' idea of placing furniture as a composition in space. Pado and Adams have included classic pieces of furniture by, of course, Mies, but also Wassily chairs by Marcel Breuer and some of Pado's own pieces made especially for this space.

Unusually, this space has a wood-burning stove. Being on the top floor allows this. It gives a focal point to the room and "is one of our favorite areas, especially during a snowfall," says Pado. This block has only single-glazed windows so the extreme heat of Chicago in the summer can really be felt.

LEFT PAGE / LOOKING DOWN THE BUILDING YOU CAN SEE ONE OF THE I BEAM DETAILS OF THE BUILDING'S FACADE.

TOP LEFT / THE VIEW UP LAKE SHORE DRIVE SHOWS THE PROXIMITY OF LAKE MICHIGAN'S BEACHES.

BOTTOM LEFT / FROM THE ROOF THERE IS A STUNNING VIEW OF THE CHICAGO SKYLINE, WITH ITS MIXTURE OF ARCHITECTURAL STYLES, IN THE DISTANCE.

TOP RIGHT / THE VIEW SOUTH CATCHES CHICAGO IN ALL ITS VARIETY: LAKE POINT TOWER, THE BUSY TEN-LANE FREEWAY, AND THE FERRIS WHEEL ON NAVY PIER.

BOTTOM RIGHT / THE ENTRANCE LOBBY OF THE LAKE SHORE DRIVE APARTMENTS IS A QUIET HAVEN AWAY FROM THE BUSTLE OF THE BUSY FREEWAY OUTSIDE.

RIGHT PAGE / FROM THE BEDROOM, THE NEXT-DOOR BUILDING CAN BE SEEN THROUGH THE VERTICAL BLINDS.

ABOVE / THE DINING AREA, WITH MIES CHAIRS SURROUNDING A PADO-DESIGNED TABLE, OVERLOOKS THE MAIN SITTING AREA. THE KITCHEN IS OFF TO THE LEFT.

LEFT PAGE / THE DINING AREA, WITH THE VERTICAL BLINDS CLOSED, CREATES A PEACEFUL AREA FOR ENTERTAINING. ON THE WALLS IS A COLLECTION OF EARLY-TWENTIETH-CENTURY GERMAN ART.

ABOVE / THE ENDLESS BAYS OF WINDOWS IN THIS TOP-FLOOR LAKE SHORE DRIVE APARTMENT ALLOW VIEWS OF THE FAR DISTANCE. TRAVERTINE FLOORING UNITES THE SPACES.

RIGHT PAGE / THE GALLEY KITCHEN IS FULLY FITTED AND HAS DRAMATIC CONCEALED LIGHTING FEATURES. IT CAN BE ACCESSED FROM EITHER END, AND HAS THE OPTION OF BEING LEFT OPEN AS A CORRIDOR OR ENCLOSED WHEN NOT IN USE.

ABOVE / THIS APARTMENT HAS BEEN ENLARGED BY ADDING SPACE FROM AN ADJOINING UNIT. THIS EXPANSION GIVES THE EXTRA BAY OF FLOOR-TO-CEILING WINDOWS. MUCH OF THE FURNITURE HERE WAS SPECIALLY DESIGNED BY MICHAEL PADO FOR THIS APARTMENT.

HIGH-RISE NOW

Now is what's happening. Now is what's new. Now is **living for today.**

High-rise Now includes a vast array of apartments and flats, whether remodeled, renovated, or restored. This section showcases places and spaces across the globe, from **London to Vancouver,** from **Hong Kong to New York.**

High-rise living has been rediscovered; **it's the place to live**—and not only for the city dweller, as this section will show. High-rise Now is **for all budgets** and schemes, from the self-designed to the architect's complete makeover. High-rise Now includes **ideas and inspirations** for those who are already high-rise dwellers and also those about to make the move.

MINI STO

ARCAND RESIDENCE, VANCOUVER

Located in Vancouver, on the twenty-third floor of a 1986 apartment block by Raffi Architects Inc. just across from Granville Island, this 1,500-square-foot condominium has been completely redesigned. The initial intention with the '80s interior of stippled ceilings, different colors in every room, and hodgepodge rooms, was to simply refresh the place with new paint and flooring.

Darren Onyskiw, the interior architect, spent two days and nights in the place, noting the space in relation to the daylight. What was initially a makeover program became a complete redesign. There was no way a simple replastering, repainting, and reflooring job would update the apartment. It needed the complete reworking of each room to ensure a successful transformation.

Doorways and openings to the rooms have been widened and heightened to capture the view from within one room to another, an incredible visual experience. With an apartment like this—180-degree, awe-inspiring views out of windows facing north, northwest, south, and southwest—the client requested that the space be opened up to let the outside come in. The removal of some walls opened up the once-den-now-dining-room to the hallway and kitchen, and gave natural light to what used to be an oppressive and uninviting entrance. The windows throughout are without drapery and blinds so there is nothing obstructing the light from coming in and the views, looking out.

Throughout the apartment natural materials are used, with the exception of the translucent Plexiglas sliding cabinet doors and the solid, hard-wearing Avonite recessed work surfaces in the kitchen area, which have been sanded to give a softness to the otherwise hardness of the plastic..Maple flooring continues throughout the entire space, and cabinetry appears to float amongst the softness of multicoated walls that have been airbrushed with a minimum of five layers of paint, enabling the wall finishes to absorb the light rather than reflect it.

The furniture selection complements the window levels in every room. Low-level seating, occasional tables, and the bed are all at the same plane as the lowest window point, affording clear views from room to room.

LEFT PAGE / THE BUILDING IS LOCATED ACROSS FROM GRANVILLE ISLAND, ONE OF VANCOUVER'S MANY ECLECTIC ATTRACTIONS.

ABOVE / THIS CONTEMPORARY VANCOUVER APARTMENT IS STREAMLINED AND FREE OF ANY UNNECESSARY DECORATION, YET FEELS LIKE HOME. THE WARMTH OF WOOD FLOORING ADDS AN IMPORTANT WELCOME TO THE SPARE SPACE.

RIGHT PAGE / THE VIEW FROM THE BAY WINDOW IN THE MAIN LIVING AREA OF ANOTHER HIGH-RISE, HANGS LIKE A PIECE OF MODERN ART.

ABOVE LEFT / THE LARGE ARTWORKS GIVE A SCALE TO THE SPACE AND SPLASHES OF COLOR TO AN OTHERWISE MONOCHROME INTERIOR. THE KITCHEN AREA CAN BE SEEN THROUGH THE FULL-HEIGHT OPENING.

LEFT PAGE / THE CONTEMPORARY FURNITURE ADDS TO THE LIGHTNESS OF THE SPACE AND FLOATING ELEMENTS OF THE WALLS AND FITTED FURNITURE.

ABOVE RIGHT / DOORWAYS WERE ALTERED AND REMOVED TO CREATE LONG VIEWS WITHIN THE APARTMENT.

WATERFRONT/BONDSUITE, HONG KONG

Edge Design Institute Ltd., fronted by Gary Chang and located in Hong Kong, has completed many schemes in high-rise buildings throughout Asia.

Titled "Waterfront/Bondsuite," this apartment is actually a duplex in West Kowloon and is flanked by the Victoria Harbor with Hong Kong Island as a backdrop.

The various spaces within the apartment have either a balcony, a bay window, or an arrangement of corner windows designed to optimize the views.

The layout creates a promenade leading from the lobby area through the dining area, to the living area, then on to the study. A staircase leads to the upper level, which houses two bedroom suites.

The decoration of the duplex, to enhance the experience of the space and its fluidity, has been carefully selected to keep a continuity between each area. A neutral silver paint was used on all the window walls, tying each window frame to the next, keeping the view uninterrupted by any stronger wall finish. The internal walls are covered with a very dark laminated wood, inlaid with copper strips that create dashes of light in the dark surface. This effect is continued throughout the entire lower level, accentuating the dramatic effect of the glass-bead wall in the dining area, which ties in the chandelier suspended above the dining table.

The overall concept of this apartment is tranquility and unity with a solid, carefully choreographed procession of space-after-space right in the hustle of Hong Kong.

RIGHT / IN DAYLIGHT THE COPPER INLAY STRIPS APPEAR TO GLOW.

ABOVE / THE CEILINGS AND WALLS ARE TREATED AS SLABS OF DECORATION TO EITHER DIVIDE OR ACCENTUATE THE SPACE. IN THE DINING AREA THEY CONCEAL THE LIGHT SOURCE.

RIGHT PAGE / THE APARTMENT'S BEADED WALL TREATMENT AND LIGHTING ARRANGEMENT REFLECT 1930s GLAMOUR.

ABOVE / THIS COMPLETELY BUILT-IN AREA, WITH ITS FINISHED SURFACES AND SYMMETRY, GIVES THE FEEL OF LIVING IN AN ART DECO HIGH-RISE.

LEFT PAGE / THE LIGHTING OF THIS SPACE CREATES AN IMMEDIATE ATMOSPHERE. YOU WILL EITHER LOVE IT OR HATE IT.

LEFT / THE WINDOWS IN DIFFERENT AREAS ARE AT DIFFERENT ANGLES. THE SILVERED WALL FINISH CONTRASTS WITH THE THE DARK WOOD VENEER OF THE STAIRCASE AND DIVIDING WALL TO THE APARTMENT, ADDING TO THE LUXURY OF THE WHOLE SPACE. COPPER INLAY GIVES AN ILLUSION OF BACKLIT ILLUMINATIONS.

HOFFMAN RESIDENCE, VANCOUVER

Vancouver's skyline is full of endless high-rise buildings, with plenty more going up around and between them.

This apartment in Vancouver's West End is a building of thirty-one floors, built in the late 1980s. The tower tapers as it rises so that the higher up in the tower, the fewer units there are on each floor.

On the fourteenth floor, a unit of some 1,500 square feet has views of English Bay: four balconies, each on a different corner, offer four different views. Originally a three-bedroom space, the apartment has been transformed into a one-bed condo with two bathrooms, a living/dining room, and a den with a pull-down bed for guests.

Having seen but being unable to buy the Arcand residence by Darren Onyskiw, owner Barry Hoffman called in the same architect to handle the renovation of his new home.

Onyskiw says, "We took the place completely apart and rebuilt as much of the interior as we could."

The apartment is a backdrop for a collection of art and furniture collected through traveling, working, and living in cities across the world. The modern elements of the total scheme act as a foil that unites the various styles and periods of the art and artifacts on display throughout the apartment. Custom-built storage blocks break up the space and hide all electrical appliances, heating appliances, and switches: a storage area on one side and a plane for art on the other.

The position of this apartment block makes it an ideal location for twenty-first-century living, being only half a block away from Vancouver's Robson Street, with more restaurants than you could wish for and several grocery stores. There are open green spaces three or four blocks away, and Stanley Park, an area of tranquility in a busy city, is only a ten-minute walk away.

RIGHT PAGE / THE BUILDING, IN VANCOUVER'S WEST END, HAS VARIOUS LAYOUTS ON EACH FLOOR. THE SEMICIRCULAR BAYS, SOME ENCLOSED AND SOME OPEN, ADD AN INTERESTING DETAIL TO THE OTHERWISE FLAT ELEVATION.

ABOVE / A TRADITIONAL-INSPIRED MODERN INTERIOR HAS BEEN FILLED WITH A WIDE COLLECTION OF FINDS AND TREASURES.

LEFT PAGE / THE TERRACE GIVES A VIEW OVER ALL NEARBY BUILDINGS. THE OPEN, CURVED, OUTDOOR SPACE IN THIS APARTMENT IS ONE OF THE ALL-IMPORTANT FEATURES OF LIVING HIGH-RISE.

TOP LEFT / AN ECLECTIC MIXTURE OF FURNITURE STYLES AND PERIODS WORKS WELL IN THIS OVERALL CONTEMPORARY SCENE.

BOTTOM LEFT / THE ULTRA-SLEEK BATHROOM HAS CONCEALED LIGHTING. THIS, ALONG WITH THE MIRROR, SERVES TO ENLARGE THE MINIMAL SPACE.

TOP RIGHT / THE LIVING AREA IS FLOODED WITH SUNLIGHT. THE USE OF TRADITIONAL RUGS BREAKS UP EACH AREA.

BOTTOM RIGHT / A GROUPING OF ANTIQUES IN A MODERN INTERIOR. THIS CONFIRMS THAT OLD AND NEW CAN WORK TOGETHER HARMONIOUSLY.

RIGHT PAGE / TYPICAL OF INTERIOR ARCHITECT DARREN ONYSKIW'S WORK, ONE ROOM LOOKS INTO THE NEXT TO TAKE ADVANTAGE OF THE BEST POSSIBLE VIEWS.

ABOVE / THE BEDROOM ON THE CORNER OF THE BUILDING HAS FLOOR-TO-CEILING WINDOWS. THE ANTIQUE WOOD FURNITURE IS A WONDERFUL CONTRAST TO THE MODERN ARCHITECTURAL FEATURES.

LEFT PAGE / THE KITCHEN AREA IS TREATED AS BUILT-IN FURNITURE. TOPPED WITH MARBLE, THE UNIT IS SET INTO STUD PARTITIONS.

MULLING RESIDENCE, NEW YORK

This tiny apartment in New York's West Village shows what you can do to make a small space feel much bigger. John Mulling, interior designer, made this space his home with a few simple alterations.

John chose this place on the seventh floor of a small block in the city, for its views and great location. The co-op apartment of just under 500 square feet has been transformed from an L-shaped studio to a flexible, one-bedroom space.

With a series of floor-to-ceiling sliding doors that can open and close areas when needed, the whole space is used. Because of the storage and shelving in every available space, the apartment works as though it were much bigger. By remodeling the whole space and relocating the kitchen entrance, John was able to create an enclosed bedroom area that can actually be closed off or left open. It has a great corner window that brings the outside in—great views of the rooftops below. John refers to the space as his "ship's cabin," where every inch of space is used to full advantage. By shifting walls and moving the kitchen area, a small office/workspace could be included. This makes the main living area a straightforward rectangle with no unnecessary details, nooks, or alcoves.

Along the length of this living area is a built-in bench, which provides much-needed storage and is a suitable display area for John's artwork and object collection. The long, low bench also tricks the eye into experiencing the apartment as longer and higher than it really is.

For the owner, this place is a private, safe haven where he can shut the door at the end of the day and leave all the exhausting elements of living in the city behind.

RIGHT PAGE / THE CURVED EXTERIOR OF THE BUILDING IN NEW YORK'S WEST VILLAGE.

ABOVE / THIS SMALL SPACE, TREATED AS A WHOLE INSTEAD OF A SERIES OF SEPARATE ROOMS, IS FILLED WITH LOW STORAGE AND SLIDING GLASS DOORS TO OPEN UP OR CLOSE OFF OTHER SPACES.

ABOVE / THE HOMEY FURNITURE AT THE FAR END OF THE APARTMENT IS WELCOMING. THE BEAUTIFUL GLASS PARTITIONS LET LIGHT PASS THROUGH TO THIS AREA FROM OTHER ROOMS.

ABOVE / THE BEDROOM CAN BE EITHER COMPLETELY EXPOSED OR HIDDEN. THE SHELVES ABOVE THE HEADBOARD SHOW HOW WELL EVERY AREA OF SPACE IS USED THROUGHOUT THIS SMALL APARTMENT.

RIGHT PAGE / THE COMFORTABLE URBAN FEEL OF THIS BATHROOM IS UNDERSCORED BY THE UNUSUAL PLACEMENT OF THE SHADED LAMP.

ROSS RESIDENCE, NEW YORK

This small, eleventh-floor apartment in New York, residence of textile designer Judy Ross and her family, looks out over an idyllic garden at high level, a reference to the ideals of the garden city of earlier times. In fact, the concept of gardens in the sky is becoming more important as more high-rises are being built.

As you enter this apartment block from a bustling city square, it's difficult to imagine what you are going to find when you arrive at the apartment; the hard-faced building with its corporate identity hides corridors of apartments at various levels.

Judy's apartment of about 600 square feet houses two bedrooms, an open-plan kitchen, and living and dining areas, all simply furnished with midcentury style. With its collection of furniture, works by fellow artists and craftsmen, and pieces by Judy herself, the home is a statement of the owners' tastes and travels.

The simple decor of polished maple floors, aluminum blinds, and white walls is timeless and works as a backdrop to the artwork and books that fill the built-in storage. Judy's travels and her great eye for detail mean that, without a doubt, some pieces will be moved out for something better when it comes along.

Because of the building's position on the corner of the block, the windows look out to the back and the side of the building. With no taller buildings at close proximity, the outlook is clear—quite surreal—with distant rooftop water reservoirs especially visible against a sunset.

With the high-level garden just out of the window, quite unusual for a high-rise apartment, especially in New York, the scenery is always changing, and it is possible to feel a connection to nature through the seasons, despite being on the eleventh floor. From the garden there are also great views of the Empire State Building; if the garden tranquility makes you forget where you are, you'll soon remember with these views.

LEFT PAGE / A COMMUNAL ROOF TERRACE AT THIS HIGH LEVEL GIVES GREAT VIEWS OF THE CITY'S LANDMARK BUILDINGS.

COMMON THREADS HALL
The Writings of Robert Smithson
Tie-dyed Textiles of India
Robert Motherwell on Paper
70s
60s
Decorative Art
DAY
50s
Decorative Art
TASCHEN
TASCHEN
Palestinian Costume
FELIX VALLOTTON
The Van Eycks
Andy Warhol
Zeichnungen 1942 – 1987
インド
沙漠の民と美
BERGMAN

ABOVE / THE LIVING ROOM INCLUDES A DINING AREA. ON ONE SIDE, A WALL OF BOOKS AND RECORD ALBUMS KEEPS EVERYTHING ORGANIZED IN ONE PLACE. ON THE FLOOR IS A RUG BY JUDY ROSS.

LEFT PAGE / THIS VINTAGE DINING SET, A CLOSE MATCH IN HEIGHT TO THE WINDOW LEDGE, ALLOWS UNINTERRUPTED VIEWS WHILE ENTERTAINING.

ABOVE / THE MAIN BEDROOM IS A SERENE RETREAT AND HOUSES A COLLECTION OF VINTAGE ITEMS AND TREASURED POSSESSIONS FROM FRIENDS AND FELLOW ARTISTS.

ABOVE / A CORNER ROOM FOR THE CHILD PROVIDES MORE SURFACES TO FILL AND COVER. THE HEATING ELEMENT IS A GREAT CANVAS FOR A COLLECTION OF FRIDGE MAGNETS.

DEFOUW RESIDENCE, NEW YORK

When actress Kathleen DeFouw bought this twenty-sixth-floor corner apartment in New York's Greenwich Village, she called in The Moderns to do the remodeling.

The Moderns' Janine James had renovated DeFouw's previous studio apartment, so DeFouw knew who to get to work on her new home. She even invited James, who came up with some great ideas, to have a look before she purchased it.

The apartment was a typical postwar high-rise with parquet flooring, an enclosed kitchen, a small bathroom, and an array of useless details that were all removed. The basic layout, and of course the views, were what initially drew DeFouw to this unit.

Living high-rise becomes part of your environment; the exterior of endless space, the views, and the peace and solitude that come with living high-rise. Moving from Los Angeles to New York, DeFouw wanted an unobstructed view: this apartment has great views, as far as Verrazano Bridge on a clear day. From here you can see the East River, Williamsburg, and the Manhattan and Brooklyn bridges. "They are beautiful at night when they are lit up," she says.

The space is treated as a whole space, rather than a series of rooms. A foyer/entrance hall was created using sandblasted Plexiglas to bring light into the area from the bedroom, which receives morning sun.

There is now an open-plan kitchen, a signature of The Moderns' work, and there is a wall of flip-down storage that is also coated with sandblasted Plexiglas, giving an otherwise stark area a kind of softness. In the main living area there is a hidden home office behind folding doors, making it easy to conceal when guests arrive.

Throughout the apartment, bamboo and slate flooring unite the different areas. Special plastering techniques have been used on the walls in the foyer/entrance and one wall in the bedroom. All the cabinetry is in cherry wood, a great contrast to the bamboo flooring.

RIGHT PAGE / A STUNNING VIEW INCLUDES THE BRIDGES OF NEW YORK. LEST YOU FORGET, THE NEXT-DOOR APARTMENT BLOCK REMINDS YOU OF WHERE YOU ARE.

Wireless

TOP LEFT / THE LIVING ROOM, WITH ITS BAMBOO FLOOR, INCLUDES A DINING AREA, AND FURNITURE BY ALVAR AALTO. BUILT-IN STORAGE DISGUISES THE HEATING ELEMENTS.

BOTTOM LEFT / THE KITCHEN AREA IS DESIGNATED WITH A DROPPED CEILING. THE USE OF CHERRY VENEER MAKES THE KITCHEN ISLAND APPEAR MORE LIKE A PIECE OF FURNITURE AND IT TIES IN WITH OTHER BUILT-IN UNITS THROUGHOUT THE APARTMENT.

LEFT PAGE / THE ENTRANCE LOBBY OF THE MAIN BUILDING ECHOES ELEMENTS OF MIES VAN DER ROHE'S IDEAS FOR THE LAKE SHORE DRIVE APARTMENTS, INCLUDING THE PLACEMENT OF THE FURNITURE WITHIN THE SPACE.

TOP RIGHT / IN THE BEDROOM, THE DEEP CLOSETS HOUSE SHOES. THE USE OF SANDBLASTED PLEXIGLAS GIVES AN ILLUSION OF SPACE AND ALLOWS LIGHT INTO OTHERWISE DARK AREAS.

BOTTOM RIGHT / THIS SPACE, TREATED AS A WHOLE INSTEAD OF BEING DIVIDED INTO DISCRETE ROOMS, INCLUDES A BUILT-IN OFFICE AND A KITCHEN ISLAND, EACH ELEMENT RELATING TO THE NEXT.

PREVIOUS PAGE (TOP) / THE LIGHT STREAMS THROUGH THE JUDY ROSS TEXTILES. THE APARTMENT INCLUDES CLASSIC PIECES OF MIDCENTURY DESIGN SUCH AS THE EAMES DCW CHAIR.

PREVIOUS PAGE (BOTTOM) / IN THE EVENING, THE APARTMENT GLOWS WITH WARM TONES. THE UNDERSTATED FORMS AND TEXTURES OF THE CHERRY WOOD BAR AND WOVEN BAR STOOLS HELP CREATE AN INVITING SPACE.

ABOVE / AT DUSK THE VIEW IS BREATHTAKING. THE VIEW OUTSIDE A HIGH-RISE IS AS IMPORTANT AS THE SPACE WITHIN.

HASTREITER RESIDENCE, NEW YORK

When the memories of your family home are the inspiration for your own grown-up home, why not actually re-create some of those elements for your own use?

Kim Hastreiter, editor of *Paper* magazine, grew up with plaid-covered, L-shaped sofas, shag-pile carpets, and classic design pieces from the '50s and '60s. For her nineteenth-floor apartment home in a midcentury block overlooking Washington Square in New York, she called in the architect who had created her mother's interior to put in those important emotional details.

Ignoring its bad layout and shabbiness, Kim moved into this apartment because of its views. The World Trade Center's twin towers were symmetrically placed in every set of windows in the place.

There are also great views of the park below, but 9-11 did change the feel of the place. "Watching the planes crash into the twin towers that morning over coffee from my living room two years ago, and then watching the buildings fall made me a nervous wreck about airplanes flying over my building and especially towards my building."

This apartment is a true extension of its owner. It is not a stage set; it is a mix of old and new put together by Kim. It is a place where she can surround herself with art, furniture, lighting, and other stuff made by her talented group of friends. She is a true collector, an obsessive gatherer.

In the apartment you can find an impressive collection of artwork by friends such as Jean-Michel Basquiat, Keith Haring, Steven Sprouse, and Barry McGee, and photographs by Nick Waplington and Martin Parr. Every surface is covered with something that relates to the next, and the kitchen cupboards are heaving with colorful pots from years of flea-market treks.

The whole place is full of color; with the off-white walls, everything has an ideal natural foil to fall against, and combined with pale wood floors and white blinds, there is brightness throughout the flat.

The added bonus of this space is a great terrace where Kim grows vegetables, from eggplants to peppers, tomatoes to figs, and where there are also continuous flowers throughout the year.

LEFT PAGE / FROM HER TERRACE, HASTREITER OVERSEES THE HISTORY OF DECADES WORTH OF HIGH-RISE BUILDINGS.

RIGHT / THE ALL-IMPORTANT TERRACE FEATURES WIRE MESH FURNITURE. KIM GROWS HER OWN VEGGIES HERE.

TOP LEFT / HASTREITER REMODELED AND OPENED UP THE APARTMENT WHEN SHE BOUGHT IT. WITH THE KITCHEN NOW OPEN TO THE BREAKFAST AREA, SUNLIGHT CAN STREAM THROUGH.

BOTTOM LEFT / THE DINING END OF THE MAIN LIVING AREA FEATURES A LARGE PAINTING BY PHIL FROST. AT THE FAR END OF THE ROOM IS A COMPLETE WALL OF HIDDEN STORAGE.

LEFT PAGE / HASTRIETER'S ABODE HOUSES THE RESULTS OF HER LIFETIME OF COLLECTING, FROM THE JACOBSEN "SERIES 7" CHAIRS, TO ART WORKS BY FRIENDS AND COLLEAGUES, TO HER TREASURED FLEA-MARKET FINDS.

TOP RIGHT / IN THE KITCHEN ARE STACKS OF COLORED POTS IN OPEN-FRONTED CABINETS. WHY HIDE YOUR COLLECTIONS?

BOTTOM RIGHT / IN THE BEDROOM, LIGHT FLOODS IN ABOVE A DAYBED LINED WITH AMPLE PILLOWS FOR COMFORT.

ABOVE / THE PLAID-UPHOLSTERED, FITTED COUCH, INSPIRED BY KIM'S FAMILY HOME, FILLS AN ENTIRE WALL. THE EAMES SURFBOARD TABLE IS FROM THE 26TH STREET FLEA MARKET.

ARANDA REDESIGN, CHICAGO

It's hard to believe that just eighteen months ago this Lake Shore Drive apartment was a late-'80s postmodern shrine to urbanism.

The present owner called in the designer/architect Mario Aranda after seeing his work in Ikram, a store in Chicago. The store's decor is created of luxury materials such as mahogany, burnished bronze, and amber glass that allow the merchandise to complement the clothing it sells—European high-end fashion—and allow the merchandise to stand out. She wanted the apartment to recapture its original spirit.

The apartment was completely gutted; everything that was not of the original 1950s plan was removed. New internal walls were installed and new finishes were applied.

This nineteenth-floor apartment was originally a three-bed/two-bath. With the removal of one wall, the living space now spreads across six window bays, giving, approximately, a thirty-foot spread of floor-to-ceiling glass.

When you first walk into this space, if you didn't already know you were in Chicago, it would be hard to guess where you were. The incredible view of very blue Lake Michigan gives the appearance of living in a beach house in Malibu or Sarasota. But then you look down and you realize you are on a busy highway. This brings you back to reality. Being a corner apartment, this space has views of the city as well. It's a great balance of views, from the peaceful endless Great Lakes blue to the up-front architecture just out of the window.

Mario Aranda's expertise for matching materials gives the place a feeling of tranquility, harmony, and luxury. Floating wall details echo the metal window frames and actually work as runners for rosewood sliding doors. The open-plan kitchen, faced with walnut veneer, creates more of a feeling of built-in furniture than a built-in kitchen.

The floor throughout the living and kitchen area is sandblasted travertine. It echoes the floor of the apartment block's main entrance lobby. Elsewhere is in an oak strip. At the entrance an archway has been formed to create an open hallway before entering. This visually breaks the space and gives a feeling of more rather than less.

This block, built a few years after 860 and 880 Lake Shore Drive, has tinted-glass windows and an overall darkness to the exterior that completes the scheme and keeps it more uniform-looking than its neighbors 860 and 880 Lake Shore Drive, where the internal window treatments are more obvious.

RIGHT PAGE / THE TWO BUILDINGS OF MIES VAN DER ROHE'S LAKEFRONT TOUR DE FORCE STAND AT RIGHT ANGLES, REFLECTING EACH OTHER.

LEFT PAGE / THE BEDROOM/DRESSING ROOM IS FULLY GLAZED, FLOOR TO CEILING. IT IS THE HEIGHT OF LUXURY TO HAVE DAYLIGHT IN THAT OFT-FORGOTTEN SPACE, THE WALK-IN WARDROBE.

PREVIOUS PAGE (LEFT) / THE GRID OF WINDOWS, A MIES INNOVATION, ALLOWS FOR THE GREATEST AMOUNT OF GLASS IN THESE APARTMENTS. THE TRAVERTINE FLOOR ECHOES THAT USED IN THE MAIN ENTRANCE LOBBY.

PREVIOUS PAGE (RIGHT) / THE ENTRANCE DOOR'S ARCHWAY CREATES MORE SPACE VISUALLY. THE WALLS HAVE A GESSO FINISH. DOORS TO THE BEDROOM AREA BALANCE OUT THE ENTRANCE.

ABOVE / THE SLEEK, CLEAN-LINED BEDROOM OVERLOOKS OTHER HIGH-RISE BUILDINGS, AND REMINDS YOU OF WHERE YOU ARE. THE OAK FLOORING WAS INSTALLED BY THE PREVIOUS OWNERS AND ACTS AS A GREAT CONTRAST TO THE HARD MATERIALS USED ELSEWHERE.

ABOVE / THE SIMPLICITY OF THIS APARTMENT'S VIEW OF BEAUTIFUL LAKE MICHIGAN IS ONLY ENHANCED BY ITS FRAME OF SLEEK FURNISHINGS AND RICH INTERIOR FINISHES.

MONTEVETRO, LONDON

Montevetro, the "glass mountain" built on the south side of the River Thames in London opposite Chelsea's Cheyne Walk, is Richard Rogers' first multihousing project in England, at a cost of about $50 million. The initial concept was put together in 1994 but not completed until 2000.

Built on a site of an old Hovis Flour mill, the triangularly shaped building flanks the riverside and is placed alongside a seventeenth-century Christopher Wren church in a park and a couple of local-authority high-rise blocks built in the 1960s.

The award-winning Montevetro is a collection of five blocks united by very obvious elevator shafts that eliminate the need for corridors to the apartments. The 103 units, ranging from 1,000 to over 2,500 square feet, and from one to four bedrooms, are at different levels due to the gentle sloping arrangement of the buildings. Each block has two double- or triple-height penthouses with floor-to-ceiling windows and views across the city, the tallest block having 360 degrees of glass.

An elevation of the building shows the layout of the apartments: the bedrooms are on the east side, and living areas and balconies on the west side. In this building all the bathrooms were prefabricated in Denmark, shipped over completed, and hoisted into place with a crane.

Montevetro also houses many services and leisure facilities for the convenience of the tenants. There are all-weather tennis courts, and saunas, and there are porters to organize your life for you, from ordering cabs to supplying maid service for that special occasion.

This penthouse apartment by Collett-Zarzycki has a mezzanine floor arrangement over the main living room. The double-height walls of glass give amazing light and spaciousness to the apartment. Every room has floor-to-ceiling walls of glass.

In this apartment there is a great deal of built-in custom storage and only the occasional piece of furniture, which retains a sense of spareness, an important key to living in this type of space. With an ever-changing vista out the window, the interior needs to be clear, uncluttered, serene, and as simple as possible. Here, furniture has been selected so as to not interfere with the exterior landscape.

The choice of interior materials and the placing of furniture and accessories give a luxurious feel to this space. The uncluttered interior combined with the use of vintage elements gives a sense of timelessness—a classic, modern environment.

RIGHT PAGE / THE FOUR BUILDINGS ARE UNITED BY ELEVATOR SHAFTS AND STAIRWELLS. EACH TOWER HAS A DOUBLE-HEIGHT UNIT AT THE TOP.

ABOVE / THE BEDROOM, SET ON A CORNER, HAS FULL-HEIGHT, UNINTERRUPTED PANES OF GLASS. SLEEPING SEEMS LIKE A WASTE OF TIME IN A BEDROOM WITH A VIEW SUCH AS THIS.

ABOVE LEFT / THE DOUBLE-HEIGHT LIVING AREA OF THIS TOP-FLOOR APARTMENT HAS A MEZZANINE FLOOR. FULL-LENGTH BLINDS BALANCE THE LIGHT LEVELS.

ABOVE RIGHT / THE STUDY IS CLEVERLY CONSTRUCTED TO PROVIDE MAXIMUM STORAGE SPACE—AN ENTIRE WALL OF IT.

PETTIGREW/WOHL RESIDENCE, CHICAGO

On the twenty-second floor of the Mies van der Rohe–designed Commonwealth Plaza building in Chicago, Paul Pettigrew, architect and professor of architecture at Illinois Institute of Technology, and his wife, Jill Wohl, copywriter and charity worker, live with their three-year-old daughter, Audrey.

Living in a high-rise is all about the view; for them the view of both Sylvan Park and the city is everything. When they had moved in after the alterations were complete, a friend visited and remarked, "I love what you've done to the view." For Paul and Jill, the 8-by-22-foot wall of glass that is their window gives them views of Lake Michigan, downtown Chicago, and the urban landscape to the west. Being on the edge of Lincoln Park, the view is unobstructed for four blocks toward the city.

Their home has been brought into the twenty-first century with contemporary sofas and dining furniture, and with Paul's adaptation of vintage furniture pieces. In the living area, a vintage George Nelson wall unit has been updated to house a workspace and appears to float in front of the glass wall.

Some alterations to the original plan were made to create a larger master bathroom and a dressing area, which both contemporizes the design and eliminates that endless hallway that plagues other apartments in the building.

Paul lives, works, and breathes Mies; his office is on Lake Shore Drive and he teaches at Crown Hall, built by Mies between 1950 and 1956.

One of the most important elements of living in this high-rise is the vertical neighborhood that exists here. There are many children in this building and instead of going down the street to visit friends, they travel up and down the elevator.

Paul and Jill have worked on the apartment design themselves, putting together vintage pieces with contemporary ones, placing their art to its best advantage and creating a home that is neither precious nor pretentious.

LEFT PAGE / THE PARK BELOW IS A VISUAL RETREAT, AN ESCAPE FROM CHICAGO'S BUSY LIFESTYLE.

ABOVE / AFTER A REMODEL BY THE PRESENT OWNERS, THIS IS A CONTEMPORARY SPACE FOR TODAY'S LIVING. IT INCLUDES A MIX OF VINTAGE AND NEW DESIGN.

ABOVE / THE GEORGE NELSON UNIT, MODIFIED BY PETTIGREW FOR HIS OWN USE, WORKS AS HIS HOME OFFICE.

ANDREWS RESIDENCE, LONDON

In South London the high-rise building is not an unusual sight. With massive rebuilding schemes abounding in the 1960s, housing estates—both local-authority and private—were built.

As this block is already elevated about 400 feet above sea level, you are in a position to see endless vistas across London and farther afield from any of the apartments.

The best views, however, are on the top floor of this nine-story building, where Simon and Melanie Andrews have lived among their midcentury treasures for four years. This block is one of seven high-rise blocks on this private estate that also contains over a hundred two- and three-story houses, and was built in the early 1960s. Built on the grounds of a large Victorian mansion, the surrounds are wonderfully landscaped with mature trees, undulating lawns, and walkways dotted with the occasional artwork or sculpture.

The owners came across this penthouse purely by accident. They have friends in the area living in some of the older Victorian housing nearby. While visiting once, they noticed a photo of what looked like a '60s modernist fireplace in an estate agent's window display. They viewed the place that housed the fireplace, fell in love with it, and made an offer the same day. It was the first place they had seen and as soon as they saw it, they knew it must be theirs.

Originally the apartment was a two-bedroom with living room, kitchen, bathroom, and a large roof terrace. Sometime during the '60s, the terrace had been incorporated into the living room, creating a much more spacious arrangement. As the entire exterior wall was now aluminum-framed glass doors, the area could still be opened up in the summer months. Also, the second bedroom had been made into a study area with a brise soleil screen between it and the main living area. As this apartment has so many details that are not in the others, it seems likely that the owners at the time must have been inspired by other places they had seen and simply incorporated these ideas into their home.

Simon and Melanie have worked on the place themselves and love hunting around flea markets and salerooms looking for the perfect light fittings and accessories for their home.

Unfortunately, the kitchen and bathroom were "modernized" in the '80s. They plan to renovate these rooms with plain and simple new products that function well and will not interfere with the overall modernity of the flat.

Most probably this estate was based on the Roehampton Estate in West London, which was, of course, derived from Le Corbusier's Ville Radieuse—created with a collection of housing alternatives, in a garden, and close to all the facilities you would ever need.

The views from this flat are perhaps the best of all the rooftop apartments looking directly at the city of London; you can see onto North London, to the west to Heathrow Airport, and much farther on a very clear day.

TOP LEFT / LIGHTING, ONE OF THE MOST IMPORTANT ELEMENTS OF ANY INTERIOR, IS OFTEN OVERLOOKED. IN THIS APARTMENT, THE LAMPSHADE WAS CHOSEN WITH CARE TO KEEP THE SPIRIT OF THE OTHER DECOR.

BOTTOM LEFT / A WALL OF GLASS ACTS AS A GREAT BACKDROP TO THE SELECTED VINTAGE FURNITURE. THE PLANTS BRING IN JUST A TOUCH OF NATURE.

TOP RIGHT / CARPET AND WOOD FLOORING DIVIDE THE LIVING AREA FROM THE BEDROOM AREA. THE EAMES ROCKER LOOKS READY FOR ACTION.

BOTTOM RIGHT / THIS ROOM WAS ORIGINALLY THE OUTSIDE TERRACE. NOW AN INSIDE SPACE, IT CAN STILL BE OPENED UP TO THE ELEMENTS TO CAPTURE THE SUN AND THE CROSS BREEZE. THE JOHN AND SYLVIA REID TABLE AND CHAIRS ARE VINTAGE, FROM THE MID-'50s.

ABOVE / THE VIEW FROM THE LIVING AREA TOWARD THE ENTRANCE LOBBY AND KITCHEN SHOWS THE ORIGINAL WOOD-STRIP FLOORING AND THE BRICK-DETAIL FIREPLACE. THE LOBBY IS LINED WITH GLASS BRICKS, PROVIDING IT WITH GREAT LIGHTING.

RIGHT PAGE / THE MAIN LIVING AREA, WITH ITS SELECTION OF VINTAGE FURNITURE AND FURNISHINGS, IS IN KEEPING WITH THE ERA OF THE BUILDING'S CONSTRUCTION. THE STORAGE WALL AND BRISE SOLEIL TO THE STUDY AREA WERE ADDITIONS BY THE ORIGINAL OWNERS.

ABOVE / A ROOM WITH A (SPECTACULAR) VIEW. THIS VIEW, FAR ABOVE THE TREETOPS, IS CAPTURED FROM THE CORNER OF THE ROOM THAT WAS ONCE THE TERRACE. WHERE ELSE COULD YOU WANT TO LIVE?

BRENNAN/SCHEDLER RESIDENCE, CHICAGO

The owners of this apartment moved into an original Mies van der Rohe space at the Commonwealth Plaza and have kept true to it. As the flat came with the original floor plan, fittings, and luckily some great pieces of midcentury furniture when they bought it, anything else they added to it would only be a bonus.

Tom Brennan, illustrator, and Ana Schedler, graphic artist, made this place their park-view residence three years ago with their four-year-old daughter, Ava.

They have used color to make this place their home. With flea-market and thrift-store finds, this space really works. It is how it should be, perhaps how it would have been when the first residents moved in. A George Nelson storage system housing the home office, Saarinen womb chair, and retro sofa make this a comfortable, familiar family home. A new, floating cork floor has been installed to unify the space, and a neutral color scheme has been selected for its period timelessness. In the kitchen, between the original base and the wall cabinets, a backsplash of multicolored glass has been installed. This complements the Higgins mobile that hangs by the floor-to-ceiling wall of glass. Because of the apartment's original layout, there is a long vista from one end of the apartment to the other that gives a sense of space and enables you to view furniture and accessories from a distance.

Originally this block was intended for the rental market, but five years after construction its apartments were designated as condominiums. Back then, the block consisted of studios, one-, two-, and three-bedroom units. Now some have been knocked together to create vast units of various shapes and sizes. Additionally, there is a swimming pool, tennis court, underground parking, and a store on-site for everything you may need.

The building, with its aluminum-clad structure and detailing, has a certain clean and pure appearance. Compared to the heavy, black steel grid of the Lake Shore Drive Apartments, these buildings have an ethereal air to them.

Overlooking the park but being fairly low in the building—on the seventh floor—this apartment has the feeling of being perched in the treetops. The view is an ever-changing backdrop, and not being so high keeps you more attached to the city. Some of the higher apartments do make you feel more isolated and vulnerable. One of the best perks of this location is that there is no chance of anything being built opposite.

RIGHT PAGE / THE VIEW ACROSS LINCOLN PARK GIVES A VISUAL BREAK TO THE SKYLINE OF CHICAGO. THE VINTAGE FURNITURE SITS ON A CORK FLOOR, AND THE HIGGINS MOBILE IN THE CORNER ADDS ANOTHER DIMENSION TO THE VIEW.

TOP LEFT / IN THE MAIN BEDROOM A GIO PONTI "SUPERLEGGERA" CHAIR ACTS AS A NIGHT STAND. BUILT-IN HEATING AND COOLING ELEMENTS RUN ACROSS THE WINDOW BAYS.

BOTTOM LEFT / THE LONG VISTA FROM ONE END OF THE APARTMENT TO THE OTHER IS AN IMPORTANT ELEMENT, AS IT UNITES THE SPACES. THE COLOR PALETTE DRAWS FROM THE NATURAL ELEMENTS.

LEFT PAGE / THE FOUR-GRID WINDOW BAY TAKES UP AN ENTIRE WALL IN THE MAIN LIVING AREA.

TOP RIGHT / BRENNAN'S DAUGHTER HAS A ROOM WITH DUAL ASPECT. WITH MIDCENTURY FURNITURE BY BERTOIA AND GEORGE NELSON, THIS IS AN ENVIABLE SPACE FOR ANY CHILD.

BOTTOM RIGHT / WHERE BETTER TO SLEEP, THAN AMONG THE TREETOPS OF CHICAGO'S LINCOLN PARK?

LUCIAN FREUD
ART OF AFRICA
CENTURY
Ponti

ABOVE / FLANKED BY A WALL OF BOOKS, THIS ROOM IS THE APARTMENT'S HUB OF ACTIVITY. THE EVER-SHIFTING LIGHT CHANGES THE ROOM FROM HOUR TO HOUR, MINUTE TO MINUTE.

HIGH-RISE FUTURE

Looking to the future, the high-rise residential building is at last being reassessed as a very suitable **alternative housing** element for the **twenty-first century and beyond.**

The high-rise will be considered in some cases a **city-within-a-city: the tower will be taller,** and it will include services, shops, entertainment, and even open space. High-rises will be built of **new and alternative methods.**

Referring to elements from the great masters of the twentieth century who had the ideas but not the technology, this chapter will show a selection of ideas, projects, and concepts designed for the future, while capturing **elements of day-to-day living,** making high-rises more appealing than they ever have been.

Today's great architects are building up and working out the solution to the world's lack of **good housing for the masses.**

Skylines around the world will be changing.

BLUEBASE.MAS, LONDON

The Modular Accommodation System (MAS) conceived by London-based practice Bluebase, reuses ideas and concepts from earlier projects such as Kisho Kurokawa's Nakagin Capsule Tower, Moshe Safdie's Habitat '67, and Paul Rudolph's project for the Graphic Arts Complex in Manhattan, all designed decades ago.

The idea of creating a "container" to live in further develops the idea of modern building methods and off-site construction. The units—steel-framed and clad with fiberglass initially—could be finished in any style to complement their surroundings or use. They would be the size of a shipping container, approximately eight feet wide, nine feet high, and forty feet long, and have windows on three sides. They would be fitted out as a yacht or railcar is, with everything built-in so as to utilize every inch of space.

The typical configuration of at least six floors creates ten units. The units would be hung on the side of a steel tower that would contain the elevator and stairs.

This housing system, while quick to assemble, would also allow for easy maintenance and relocation. You could just unhook the unit from the tower and move to anywhere else there is another. While any work on the unit was being carried out—a refit for instance—a courtesy unit could be supplied while your own unit was being worked on.

This plan would fulfill the requirements for the low-cost, inner-city housing that is in such demand. A ten-unit block would cost approximately $750,000, with each unit costing about $50,000 to supply and fit out.

Bluebase envisions its MAS concept being used throughout the world, perhaps with different-size units for different locations. You would be able to move your home wherever you wanted to be, from London to Paris, in hours.

RIGHT PAGE / ONE OF THE MAIN ATTRACTIONS OF THIS PLAN WOULD BE THAT THE UNITS COULD BE MOVED RELATIVELY EASILY FROM ONE LOCATION TO ANOTHER. EACH TOWER WOULD HOUSE TEN UNITS HUNG FROM THE CENTRAL SUPPORT THAT WOULD INCLUDE THE ELEVATOR AND STAIRWELL.

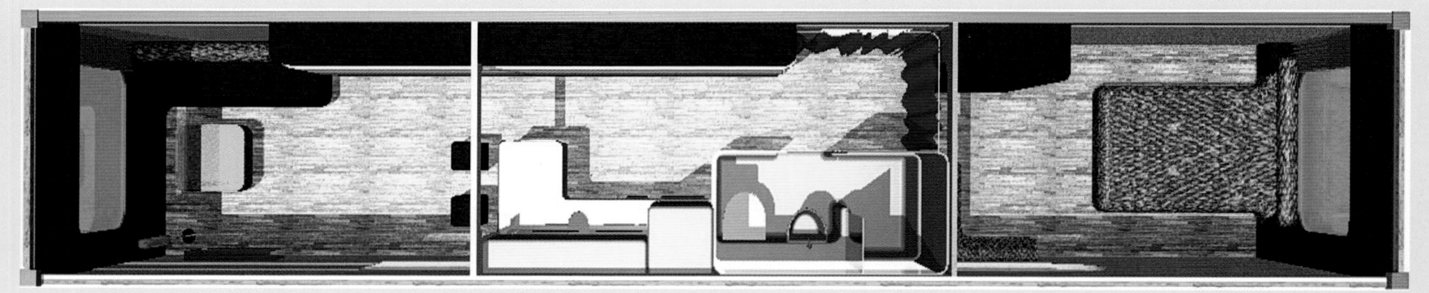

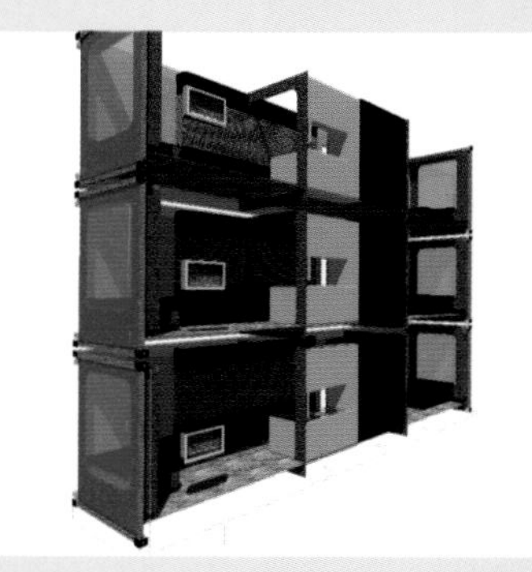

TOP / A TYPICAL SHIPPING CONTAINER, THE SAME DIMENSIONS AS THE UNIT USED FOR THIS PROJECT.

MIDDLE / A TYPICAL PLAN AND LAYOUT: ROOM FOR ALL THE ESSENTIALS.

BOTTOM / ONE OF THE REASONS A PLAN LIKE THIS WOULD BE AFFORDABLE IS THAT THE LAYOUT OF EACH UNIT WOULD BE IDENTICAL.

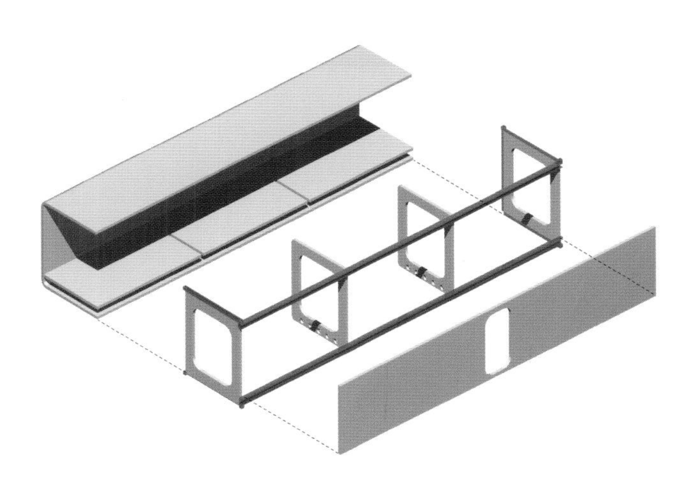

THIS PAGE / MUCH LIKE A YACHT, EACH UNIT WOULD INCLUDE A FITTED KITCHEN AS WELL AS BATHROOM, LIVING, AND SLEEPING AREAS.

THE ECO TOWER, LONDON

The Eco Tower scheme, for an area of over 180 acres in South London, is a joint venture by T. R. Hamzah and Yeang in Malaysia and London-based firm HTA Architects.

The project would consist of three towers, one of thirty-five stories and the other two of twelve stories each, to include over one million square feet of retail and leisure facilities, 3,500 new homes for the private sector for sale, over 1,000 public housing units, a new public transport interchange, a half-million square feet of office space, a hotel, accommodation for key workers such as nurses and teachers, new community facilities, and three large parks, one of which would be at least fifteen square acres.

This concept of a "city in the sky" would integrate residents of all socioeconomic levels within the same environment. The plan calls for vertical zoning; that is, different types of housing would be grouped. For example, single-occupant units would be on one floor and family units on another. The parks and shopping areas would be for everyone, as would be a regular mall and open space. The shops would be easily accessed from within the buildings, probably located at ground level. The open spaces would be landscaped and would include parks, entrance courts to different areas, and in some cases, private balconies.

One of the main innovations of the building would be to create a self-contained, large-scale urban energy system that would alternate between passive and active modes. During the passive mode, one that would work without any electro-mechanical process, the building's southerly aspect would maximize passive solar gain and heat communal areas by catching the winter sun. The internal spaces and walkways would help create lightwells that would brighten up the service areas in the apartments. The landscaping and planting throughout the scheme would act as windscreens in winter and solar screens during the summer. During the productive mode, the building would create its own energy on-site using a Photovoltaic system that would be developed according to cost.

RIGHT PAGE / AN ARTISTIC RENDERING OF THE BUILDING, SHOWING THE PARK SETTING AND THE CLOSE PROXIMITY TO LOCAL TRANSPORT.

ABOVE / THE BUILDING'S SKELETON STRUCTURE WOULD ALLOW FOR THE MOST POSSIBLE LIGHT TO PASS THROUGH THE BUILDING. THE GARDENS AT DIFFERENT LEVELS WOULD CREATE MEETING AND LEISURE AREAS.

ABOVE / THIS MODEL SHOWS THE INTERNAL STRUCTURE, INCLUDING THE HOUSING UNITS.

SKYHOUSE, LONDON

The London Eye is widely regarded as one of the great modern structures of the twenty-first century. Now the architects behind this famous glass revolving-wheel have designed a skyscraper apartment block higher than the Eiffel Tower. It is a sure sign that cities in the sky are a very real proposition for the future.

"The idea came about," says David Marks, "as a way of handling the lack of affordable housing in London." Founded by husband-and-wife team David Marks and Julia Barfield, the firm (Marks Barfield Architects, or MBA) wanted to reinvent the tower block.

"We had all learned from the bad reactions in the '60s and '70s, but now it is technically possible to do something quite wonderful."

The ideas they have planned certainly do promise to fulfill these expectations.

The team looked at the way, by necessity, an office block has to be constructed. Certain areas require a higher amount of power at specific times of the day and there has to be a great number of facilities like elevators and washrooms. But the essential cores at the centers of office buildings often make them look bulky and cumbersome.

The apartment block is a different proposition. Because of the lower density and fewer necessary utilities, you can create a very slender building for residential use. MBA has designed three elliptical towers of differing heights, the tallest with some seventy-two stories. They would be joined together so they would provide structural support for each other. The slender towers would be split into three sections of differing heights to provide communal links to all three buildings.

The echoes of Le Corbusier's Unité d'Habitation within Skyhouse—the communal areas/services at different levels, the rooftop open spaces, and self-contained-city structure—cannot be ignored. The links, two stories high, would include green spaces and meeting areas. Shops, health clubs, nurseries, and restaurants would also be included in each building.

The social implications of the Skyhouse are as forward thinking as Le Corbusier's plans for ideal city living. It is planned to house a mix of privately owned apartments, affordable housing for teachers, nurses, and other key workers, and live/work units for the growing number of people working from home.

LEFT / A CENTRAL ELEVATOR SHAFT CORE WILL UNITE THE BUILDINGS AT DIFFERENT LEVELS.

CENTER / THERE WILL BE AMPLE COMMUNAL AREAS AT DIFFERENT LEVELS, CREATING LOCAL NEIGHBORHOODS IN THE SKY. WATER SERVICES WILL BE HANDLED ON-SITE, INCLUDING RECYCLING AND TREATMENT. THE POSITIONING OF THE BUILDINGS WILL ENABLE THE MAXIMAL USE OF SOLAR ENERGY. GREEN SPACE AREAS, BOTH OPEN AND CLOSED, WILL BE INCLUDED WITHIN EACH BUILDING.

RIGHT / THREE CONNECTED TOWERS OF DIFFERENT HEIGHTS CREATE THIS CITY-WITHIN-A-CITY.

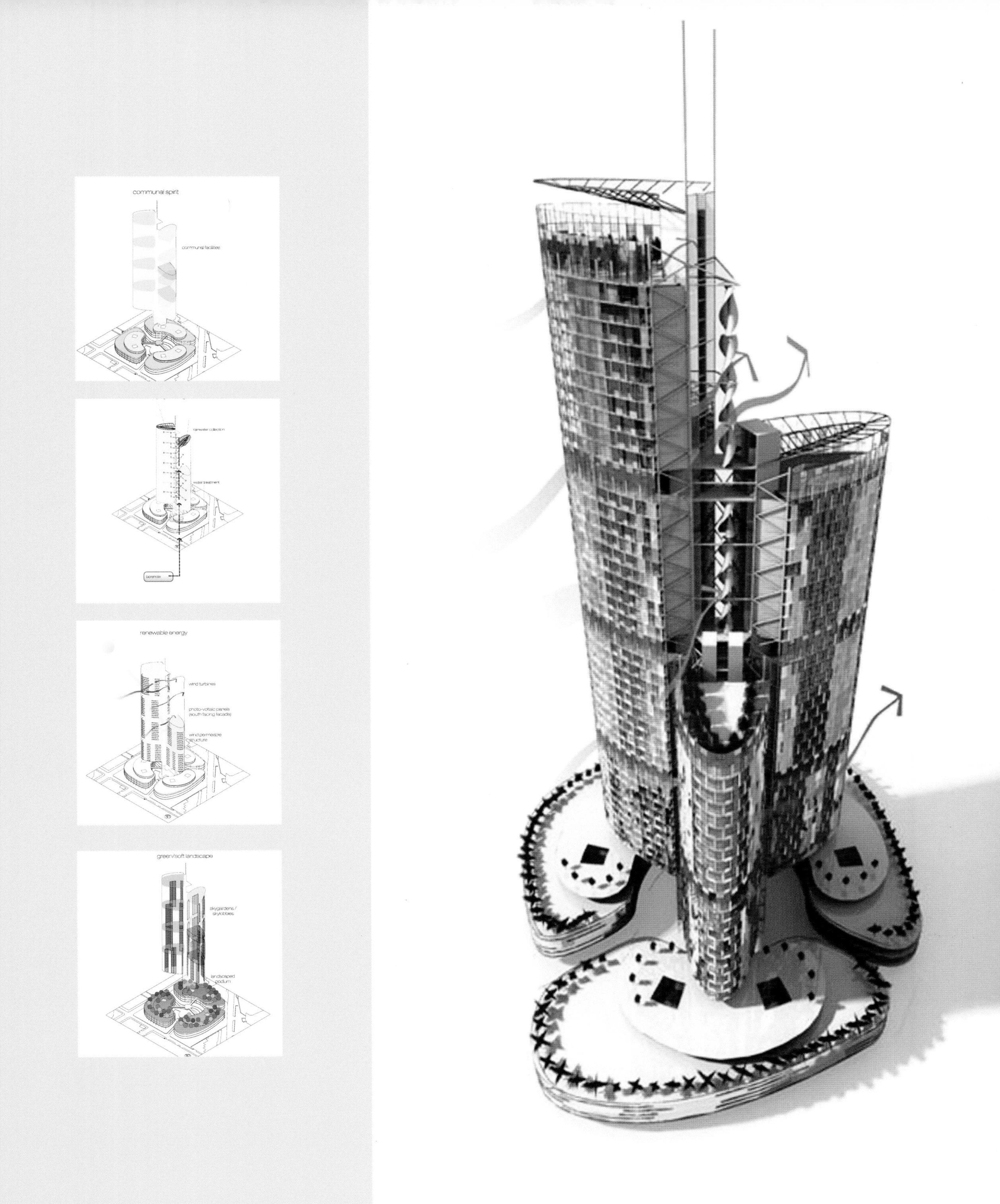
communal spirit
communal facilities
rainwater collection
water treatment
borehole
renewable energy
wind turbines
photo-voltaic panels (south facing facade)
wind permeable structure
green/soft landscape
skygardens / skylobbies
landscaped podium

ABOVE / A TYPICAL STUDIO APARTMENT, WHICH WOULD INCLUDE A SLIDING PARTITION GRANTING THE SPACE FLEXIBILITY.

ABOVE / A DOUBLE-HEIGHT APARTMENT WILL HAVE PANORAMIC VIEWS OF THE SURROUNDING CITY.

ABOVE / AN ARCHITECTURAL RENDERING SHOWS HOW A HIGH-LEVEL GARDEN AND COMMUNAL SPACE AT THE TOP OF THE BUILDING WOULD CREATE AN ESCAPE FROM CITY PRESSURES.

PRECEDING OVERLEAF / LEISURE FACILITIES INCLUDING SWIMMING POOLS WILL BE AVAILABLE TO THE RESIDENTS.

BIBLIOGRAPHY

Allan, John. *Berthold Lubetkin.* London: Merrell, 2002.

Blake, Peter. *Architecture for the New World: The Work of Harry Seidler.* Australia: Horwitz Australia Wittenborn, 1973.

Blaser, Werner. *Mies van der Rohe, Lake Shore Drive Apartments: High-rise Buildings, Wohnhochhaus.* Basel, Switzerland: Birkhauser Verlag, 1999.

Britton, Karla. *Auguste Perret.* Boston: Phaidon Press, 2001.

Bullock, Nicholas. *Building the Post War World: Modern Architecture and the Reconstitution of Britain.* New York: Routledge, 2003.

Bush-Brown, Albert. *Skidmore, Owings and Merrill, Architecture and Urbanism 1973-83.* Surrey Hills, Australia: Van Nostrand Reinhold, 1984.

Cantacuzino, Sherbin. *Wells Coates, a Monograph.* United Kingdom: Gordon Fraser, 1978.

Canrell, Michael. *I. M. Pei, Mandarin of Modernism.* New York: Clarkson Potter, 1995.

Coe, Peter. *Lubetkin and Tecton: Architecture and Social Commitment: A Critical Study.* London: Triangle Architectural Publications, 1992.

Collymore, Peter, and Ralph Erskine. *Architecture of Ralph Erskine.* Philadelphia, Pennsylvania: Coronet Books, 1990.

Cruells, Bartomeu. *Ricardo Bofill.* Barcelona: Gustavo Gili, 1995.

Egelius, Mats. *Ralph Erskine, Architect.* Philadelphia, Pennsylvania: Coronet Books, 1990.

Elwall, Robert. *Erno Goldfinger.* United Kingdom: Academy Editions, 1996.

Foerster, Wolfgang. *Harry Seidler: Social Housing—Innovative Architecture.* New York: Prestel USA, 2002.

Gans, Deborah. *The Corbusier Guide.* New York: Princeton Architectural Press, 1998.

Hall, Edward T. *The Hidden Dimension.* New York: Anchor, 1990.

Heathcoate, David. *Barbican: Penthouse over the City.* United Kingdom: Academy Editions, 2004.

Heinz, Thomas A. *Frank Lloyd Wright Interiors.* United Kingdom: Academy Editions, 1994.

Heinz, Thomas A. *Frank Lloyd Wright Public Buildings.* New York: Gramercy, 2002.

Hoffman, Donald. *Frank Lloyd Wright, Louis Sullivan and the Skyscraper.* New York: Dover Publications, 1998.

Howey, John. *The Sarasota School of Architecture.* Cambridge, Massachusetts: MIT Press, 1995.

Images Publishing Group. *Skidmore, Owings and Merrill.* Vol. 7, Master Architect Series. Victoria, Australia: Images Publishing Group, 1997

James, Warren A. *Ricardo Bofill, Building Projects 1960–85.* New York: Rizzoli, 1988.

Jenkins, David. *Unité d'Habitation.* Boston: Phaidon Press, 1993.

Johnson, Philip, and John Cook. *Conversations with Architects.* Texas: Holt, Rinehart and Winston, 1975.

Jones, Peter Blundell. *Hans Scharoun, a Monograph.* Boston: Phaidon Press, 1995.

Kirsch, Karin. *The Weissenhofseidlung: Experimental Housing Built for the Deutscher Werkbund, Stuttgart, 1927.* New York: Rizzoli, 1989.

Larkham, P. J. (ed.), and J. W. R. Whitehand. *Urban Landscape, International Perspectives.* New York: Routledge, 1992.

McNulty, Elizabeth. *Chicago Now and Then.* Berkeley, California: Thunder Bay Press, 2000.

Mies van der Rohe, Ludvig. *The Presence of Mies.* New York: Princeton Architectural Press, 1994.

Ravetz, Alison. *Council Housing and Culture.* New York: Routledge, 2001.

Schildt, Goran. *Alvar Aalto Masterworks.* New York: Rizzoli, 1994.

Schulze, Franz. *The Mies van der Rohe Archive.* London: Garland Science, 1993.

Seidler, Harry. *Harry Seidler: Selected and Current Work.* Victoria, Australia: The Images Publishing Group, 1997.

Siry, Joseph. *Carson Pirie & Scott, Louis Sullivan and the Chicago Department Store.* Chicago Architecture and Urbanism. Chicago: University of Chicago Press, 1998.

Thomson, Iain. *FLW: A Visual Encyclopedia.* Berkeley, California: Thunder Bay Press, 2000.

Unité d'Habitation: Le Corbusier Archive vol. XVII. London: Garland Publications, 1982-84.

Warburton, Nigel. *Erno Goldfinger, The Life of an Architect.* New York: Routledge, 2004.

Wilson, Richard Guy, and Sara A. Butler. *Buildings of Virginia: Tidewater and Piedmont.* New York: Oxford University Press, 2002.

Wiseman, Carter. *I. M. Pei, A Profile in American Architecture.* New York: Abrams, 2001.

Weston, Richard. *Alvar Aalto.* Boston: Phaidon Press, 1995.

RESOURCES

INFORMATION ABOUT BUILDINGS FEATURED IN CLASSIC HIGH-RISE

Frank Lloyd Wright

Price Tower
510 Dewey Avenue
Bartlesville, OK
U.S.A.

Price Tower Arts Center
www.pricetower.org

Price Tower Hotel
www.pricetowerhotel.com

Johnson Wax Building
S. C. Johnson and Son, Co.
Research Tower
Racine, WI
U.S.A.

Frank Lloyd Wright Foundation
www.franklloydwright.org

Frank Lloyd Wright Home and Studio Foundation
www.wrightplus.org

Berthold Lubetkin

Highpoint I and II
North Hill
London, N6
U.K.
www.architecture.com

Sivill House
Columbia Road
London, U.K.

Bertrand Goldberg

Marina City
State Street
Chicago, IL
U.S.A.
312.661.0046
www.architecture.org for tour details

Ludvig Mies van der Rohe

Lake Shore Drive Apartments
860–880 Lake Shore Drive
Chicago, IL
U.S.A.

Lake Shore Drive Apartments
900–920 Lake Shore Drive
Chicago, IL
U.S.A.
www.architecture.org
for tours

Commonwealth Plaza
310 W Diversey Street
Chicago, IL
U.S.A.

Kisho Kurokawa

Nakagin Capsule Tower
www.kisho.co.jp
kurokawa@kisho.co.jp

Chamberlain, Powell and Bon

Barbican Centre
Silk Street
London
WC, U.K.
www.barbicanliving.com
www.barbicanartscentre.co.uk

Golden Lane Estate
Fann Street
London
WC, U.K.

Le Corbusier

Unité d'Habitation
280 Boulevard Michelet
Marseille
France

Hotel Corbusier
280 Boulevard Michelet
Marseille
France
+33 (0) 491771815
fondationlecorbusier@wanadoo.fr

Unités are also found in Meaux and Briey en Foret, France, and Berlin-Charlottenburg, Germany.

Frank Folsom Smith

folsom@gte.net

Plymouth Harbor
700 John Ringling Boulevard
Sarasota, FL
U.S.A.
941.365.2600
sarasotaarchfndn@aol.com
for tours

Harry Seidler and Associates

www.seidler.net.au

Blues Point Tower
McMahon's Point
Sydney
Australia

Horizon Apartments
Darlinghurst
Sydney
Australia

INFORMATION ABOUT BUILDINGS FEATURED IN INTRODUCTION

Auguste Perret

Apartments at 25 bis rue Franklin
Paris, France

Louis Sullivan

Carson Pirie and Scott Department Store
1 State Street
Chicago, IL
U.S.A.
312.641.8000
www.caf.com for tours

Ludvig Mies van der Rohe

Weissenhof Seidlung
Stuttgart, Germany
www.weissenhofseidlung.de

Wells Coates

Embassy Court
Kings Road
Brighton
E Sussex
U.K.

London County Council

Housing at Roehampton
Alton West Estate
Roehampton Lane
London
U.K.

Erno Goldfinger

Balfron Tower
Rowlett Street
Poplar
London
U.K.
www.architecture.com

Ralph Erskine

Byker Wall Housing
Newcastle upon Tyne
U.K.
www.erskine.se
erskine@erskine.se

Schipporeit and Heinrich

Lake Point Tower
505 North Lakeshore Drive
Chicago, IL
U.S.A.
312.621.4610

I. M. Pei

Kips Bay Plaza
between 30-33rd Street and 1st and 2nd Avenue
New York City, NY
U.S.A.
www.pcfandp.com

Ricardo Bofill

Les Arcades du Lac
Saint-Quentin-en-Yvelines
Paris
France
www.bofill.com

Alvar Aalto

www.alvaraalto.fi

Neue Vahr
Otto-Suhr-Strasse
Berliner Freiheit
Bremen, Germany

Hans Scharoun

Romeo and Juliet Buildings
Stuttgart
Germany

Skidmore, Owings and Merrill

John Hancock Center
875 North Michigan Avenue
Chicago, IL
U.S.A.
312.751.3680
observation deck:
312.787.3800

www.som.com

www.caf.com for tour information

FEATURED ARCHITECTS AND DESIGNERS

Mario Aranda, Chicago
marioaranda@sbc.global.net

John Mulling, New York
jmulling@interiorarchitects.com

Darren Onyskiw, Vancouver
donyskiw@direct.ca

Michael Pado, Chicago
fax: 312.787.3125
Powell and Kleinschmidt, Chicago
312.642.6450
www.powellkleinschmidt.com

Paul Pettigrew, Chicago
paulpettigrew@alum.mit.edu

Larry Converso, Chicago
www.conversomod.com
conversomod@yahoo.com

The Moderns, New York
www.themoderns.com

Judy Ross, New York
judyrosstextiles@aol.com

Gary Chang, Hong Kong
www.edge.hk.com

Collett-Zarzycki, London
www.collett-zarzycki.com

Marks Barfield, London
www.marksbarfield.com

Bluebase, London
www.bluebase.com

HRA/Ken Yeang,
London/Malaysia
www.hra.co.uk

Richard Rogers and Partners, London
www.rrp.co.uk

HTA, London
www.hta-arch.co.uk

WEB SITES FOR GOOD, GENERAL INFORMATION ON HIGH-RISE ARCHITECTURE

www.greatbuildingsonline.com
www.galinsky.com
www.chicago.com
www.skyscraper.com
www.architecture.org
www.architecture.com

PHOTO CREDITS

All photography © Ray Main / Mainstream except:

Buildarchiv Foto Marburg: pages 11, left, 12

Chicago Landmark Commission: page 10

George Czerna, courtesy of Pei, Cobb, Freed and Partners: page 19

Ralph Erskine: page 22

Galinsky.com: pages 14, 34, 36, 37

Matthias Hamm: pages 157, 159, 160, 161

Peter Blundell Jones: page 17, center

Katsuhisa Kida: page 136

Courtesy of Gene Leedy: page 20, left

Courtesy of Kisho Kurokawa: pages 21, right, 52, 54, 55

Sam Lambert / Architectural Press: pages 26, 28, 29

Pierre Larauza and Antony Kwok: pages 86, 88–92

Marks Barfield Architects: pages 166, 167, 168, 169, 170, 171, 172, 173

Michele Merckling / Alvar Aalto Museum: page 17, left

Merryweather Photography: pages 38, 42, 43

Peter Cook Archigram: page 20, center

Royal Institute of British Architects Photo Library: pages 13, 15

Courtesy of Moshe Safdie and Associates: page 20, right

Harry Seidler and Associates: pages 17, right, 30, 32

Frank Folsom Smith: pages 44, 46, 47

Ben Stalling: pages 11, right, 40, 41

Martin Tessler: pages 80, 82–85, 95–101

Deidi von Schaewen: page 21, left

Morley von Sternberg: pages 48, 50, 51

Ken Yeang with HTA Architects LTD: pages 163, 164, 165